**IMPLEMENTING ELECTRONIC DATA
INTERCHANGE TO PROVIDE IN-TRANSIT
VISIBILITY**

AIR FORCE INSTITUTE OF TECHNOLOGY

Acknowledgments

Many people deserve my deep appreciation for their contributions to this research paper. At the United States Transportation Command, I would like to thank Colonel Raymond Hebert, USTRANSCOM, J4-LP, for sponsoring my research. I also want to thank the following for their time, support, and exceptional efforts in the research and review of this project: Lt Col Thomas Black, Maj Richard MacKeen, Mr. Bruce Bowman, Mr. Jim Donovan, and Mr. Ron Freed. By answering numerous questions and giving me their valuable time, they provided the support and expert knowledge this project required.

I would also like to recognize the invaluable research support provided by Ms. Janice Missildine without whom this paper would have never been possible. I am also grateful for the assistance of my AFIT research advisor, Dr. David K. Vaughan. His advice and exceptional editing abilities greatly improved my writing.

Finally, I would like to thank my wife, our daughter and son for putting up with me during the 13 month ASAM program. They continue to be my source of strength and inspiration. Although they have yet to receive any accolade or medal for their sacrifices, they know I honor them in my heart everyday.

Mark S. Danigole

Table of Contents

List of Figures

List of Tables

AFIT/GMO/ENA/00E-03

Abstract

Computers, information systems, and communications systems are being used in the transportation industry to replace cumbersome, paper-based communications processes. In every US contingency, the lack of visibility over troop movements and cargo shipments has limited the military's ability to effectively conduct operational plans. Current Department of Defense (DoD) initiatives provide some level of in-transit visibility (ITV), but are we using effective tools to gain ITV of all DoD assets within the Defense Transportation System (DTS)? The purpose of this study is to address the ITV issues and concerns that exist with gaining visibility of commercially transported DoD personnel and equipment. This study highlights the operating procedures and systems used by the DoD to electronically interface with commercial information systems to provide complete ITV.

This analysis concludes that the *Defense Transportation Electronic Data Interchange (DTEDI) Program Implementation Plan* provides an avenue for commercial shipment data collection and establishes a means by which this information is made available to Global Transportation Network (GTN) users. However, data errors and technology changeover, exacerbated by uncertain Congressional funding levels, provide barriers to DTEDI program efforts.

IMPLEMENTING ELECTRONIC DATA INTERCHANGE TO PROVIDE INCREASED IN-TRANSIT VISIBILITY

I. Overview

Theory

If an organization is to achieve its goals in an efficient manner, it must use its resources wisely. These resources include human, financial, physical, and information (Griffin, 1999: 7). This principle, applied to the Department of Defense (DoD) and the Defense Transportation System (DTS), implies that for United States Transportation Command (USTRANSCOM) to realize its goal of complete In-transit Visibility (ITV), it must use all aspects of the DTS in an efficient manner, to include DoD and commercial transportation assets.

In this study, I examine the military use of Electronic Data Interchange (EDI) to provide USTRANSCOM ITV of commercially transported DoD logistical resources. Specifically, for purposes of this study, I define my independent variable as the EDI, and my dependent variable as ITV. In other words, as EDI use increases, a change in USTRANSCOM's ability to maintain accountability of commercially transported resources is expected.

Background

Operations Desert Shield and Desert Storm required an unprecedented rapid movement of personnel and supplies from the continental United States to the Middle East Theater of operations. James Matthews, in his book *So Many, So Much, So Far, So Fast*, observed that, "In contemporary terms, the command moved to the Persian Gulf area, via air and sea, the rough equivalent of Atlanta, Georgia—all its people and their clothing, food, cars, and other belongings—half way around the world in just under seven months." Although transportation personnel were able to meet this increased logistical challenge, their success was tempered by the lack of ITV of personnel and cargo moving into and out of the area of responsibility (DoD, 1995a: 3-27). More than 20,000 of 40,000 containers entering the theater had to be stopped, opened, inventoried, resealed, and reentered into the transportation system. The effect of these inefficiencies was the unnecessary delay of time-sensitive cargo to the soldier in the field, and an estimated $150 million paid for the storage and detention of cargo containers (DoD, 1995a: 1-1).

Following Operation Desert Storm, the DoD underwent a massive reorganization. This restructuring aimed at reducing inefficiencies throughout each branch of the armed forces, and marked the beginning of a new era of military strategy. Our military strategy shifted from one of *forward presence* to one of *force projection*. The philosophy was that we would reduce our military footprint around the globe by reducing the number of permanent military facilities occupied on friendly foreign soil, and thereby create an efficient, cost-effective military force. One disadvantage of this stateside consolidation of assets was the loss of a large portion of the DoD's ability to preposition large amounts of equipment and personnel close to the anticipated battlefield. This new strategy of *force projection* forced the DoD to reexamine the DTS and develop a system that would support our new National Military Strategy and avoid the logistical problems identified in Desert Storm.

Although the problem of tracking logistical assets existed long before Operation Desert Storm, it was this shift to a *force projection* strategy that provided the impetus for an increased focus on ITV. According to James Miller, ITV is achieved "by capturing information on each shipment at its point of origin, and updating this status as assets process through each node of the transportation system."

The vast quantities of information required to maintain ITV and the speed with which this information must be available led USTRANSCOM to the development of a new ITV computer network. The Global Transportation Network (GTN) is the computer network envisioned by USTRANSCOM to be the primary ITV system. Matthews describes the GTN as a system "designed to collect, consolidate, and integrate the status and location of military cargo, passengers, patients, and lift assets from multiple DoD and commercial transportation systems" (Matthews, 1996: 28).

Another outgrowth of the military drawdown following the culmination of Operation Desert Storm was the increased reliance upon civilian owned and operated transportation assets. According to an official in the In-transit Visibility Branch, Headquarters USTRANSCOM, "The DoD has significantly increased its reliance on commercial carriers for its transportation requirements to the point where commercial carriers transport 80% of all DoD cargo" (Mackeen, 1999).

To ensure complete accountability of all commercially transported DoD resources, Electronic Data Interchange has been implemented. EDI is an application of computer technology that is moving both private and public business sectors from a paper-based accounting system to a system based solely upon electronic transactions (Payne and Anderson, 1991). It is intended that EDI will provide visibility of all commercially transported DoD cargo and personnel through the GTN, thus providing USTRANSCOM the required ITV.

Research Question

The question this study proposes to answer is: "How does Electronic Data Interchange implementation affect In-transit Visibility?" The answer to this question will determine how well the DTS is prepared to handle another "Desert Storm" type of conflict, and will facilitate understanding what changes must occur to effectively join military and commercial logistics activities in the DTS.

Investigative Questions

To answer this research question, five subsidiary questions must be answered.

1. The first step in answering the research question is to provide the reader with a fundamental understanding of Electronic Data Interchange and how it is used in the civilian sector. The first investigative question that must be answered then is, What is Electronic Data Interchange?

2. Another integral aspect of the research question is the concept of In-transit Visibility. Adding a fundamental understanding of EDI to an understanding of ITV provides the basic tools for understanding the larger issues confronting USTRANSCOM's ITV initiatives. Therefore, the second investigative question is, What is In-transit Visibility, and how does the Global Transportation Network provide it?

3. In the past, poor quality data and the absence of timely data contributed adversely to an inadequate ITV system. EDI offers the capability to correct these shortcomings and provide ITV of DoD's commercial movements via GTN. Does the DoD need ITV of commercial movements, and therefore need EDI for DTS effectiveness?

4. Even after GTN is fully developed and required system interfaces are in place, the risk of inadequate ITV information is still present. If the DoD is going to use EDI to facilitate ITV of commercially transported DoD assets, a detailed plan must be established describing a systematic approach to EDI implementation. What is the current plan for Defense Transportation EDI (DTEDI) implementation?

5. The final investigative question addresses the ability of the DTEDI program to affect ITV. What are the barriers affecting Electronic Data Interchange implementation?

Research Design and Methodology

To answer these investigative questions and ultimately answer the research question, this paper used a variety of resources. Sources of information included literature searches and personal interviews.

It is important to first define what is meant by the terms EDI and ITV. This information is found in Defense Technical Information Center (DTIC) publications, Air Force Institute of Technology resources, and the USTRANSCOM library. In addition, the researcher conducted face-to-face and telephone interviews with EDI and ITV subject matter experts resident on the USTRANSCOM staff.

Next, the researcher used personal interviews to determine how much DoD cargo and personnel are currently moved on an annual basis by commercial carriers, and how these numbers have changed since Desert Storm. Military and civilian government employees as well as government paid contractors assigned to USTRANSCOM provided required documents and personal interviews enabling collection of this data. Finally, through literature review and in-depth personal interviews, the researcher was able to determine existing barriers that impede EDI implementation.

Contributions to Theory and Practice

USTRANSCOM is charged with the management and accountability of all DoD transportation assets encompassing the DTS. With shrinking budgets reducing our nation's transportation capabilities, DTS must increase its reliance upon commercial carriers to maintain a minimum transportation capability.

My proposed research topic, "How does Electronic Data Interchange implementation affect In-transit Visibility?" explores USTRANSCOMs ability to account for all commercially transported assets. Without ITV of its commercially transported assets, the DoD cannot have ITV of all transported equipment and personnel and is likely to repeat mistakes committed during Operation Desert Shield/Storm.

II. EDI and ITV Overview

Chapter Overview

With declining defense budgets and the shift in our nation's National Defense Strategy from *forward presence* to *force projection*, the Department of Defense (DoD) is forced to explore alternatives that improve operational efficiency and effectiveness in the Defense Transportation System.   The purpose of this chapter is to explain what is meant by the terms Electronic Data Interchange, In-transit Visibility, and the Global Transportation Network (GTN). Additionally, the link between EDI and ITV is established.

Electronic Data Interchange

Efficient and reliable communications are critical capabilities for all organizations to possess in today's high-technology business environment. During the past ten years, the proliferation of cellular phones, personal computers, and the Internet has enabled virtually anyone to achieve instant access to information anywhere in the world with the touch of a button. Electronic Data Interchange (EDI) is a natural progression of society's increased dependence on technology and the ability of technology to improve inter-organizational communications.

Electronic Data Interchange Definition. The *Defense Intransit Visibility Integration Plan* defines EDI as "The computer-to-computer exchange of data from common business documents using standard data formats" (DoD, 1997: B-1). Meier discusses the three key aspects of this definition in *The Implementation of Electronic Data Interchange (EDI) With Defense Transportation Operations*: (Meier, 1994: 8)

- Computer-to-computer: Once the data is entered into the originator's application, the information flows directly to the receiver's application. The key point is that once entered, the data flows between organizations without human intervention and without paper.

- Business documents: Information that is currently found on any business form is appropriate for EDI. Examples of typical business documents which are exchanged electronically include: purchase orders, invoices, bills of lading, status reports, receipt acknowledgements, and payment information.

- Standard data format: As discussed, EDI is the electronic exchange of information from one computer to another without human intervention. For this to occur the data must be precisely formatted to allow computers to both read and understand the information.

EDI is not a specific system; it is an application of existing and emerging technologies that provides for the sharing of data between organizations. EDI is an efficient and effective means of doing business in today's high-technology business environment.

Purpose of Electronic Data Interchange. EDI improves the efficiency and accuracy of inter-organizational communications by eliminating paper-based transactions and replacing them with pure electronic communications. According to Meier, "This is accomplished through the use of established standards which provide the required structured format (language), allowing direct data transmission from one organization's computer to another organization's computer without human intervention" (Meier, 1994: 9). Figure 1 and Figure 2 illustrate the difference between a traditional paper-based data-sharing system and an EDI system.

As shown in Figure 1, the traditional system requires numerous individual operations and human intervention to accomplish the data-sharing task. The sending organization must first input data into its own computer system and upload this information to the organization's central storage system, possibly a mainframe computer. Once uploaded to the central storage system, the information is available to any authorized individual. To share the information with other external organizations, the sending organization must

Paper Based Distribution System

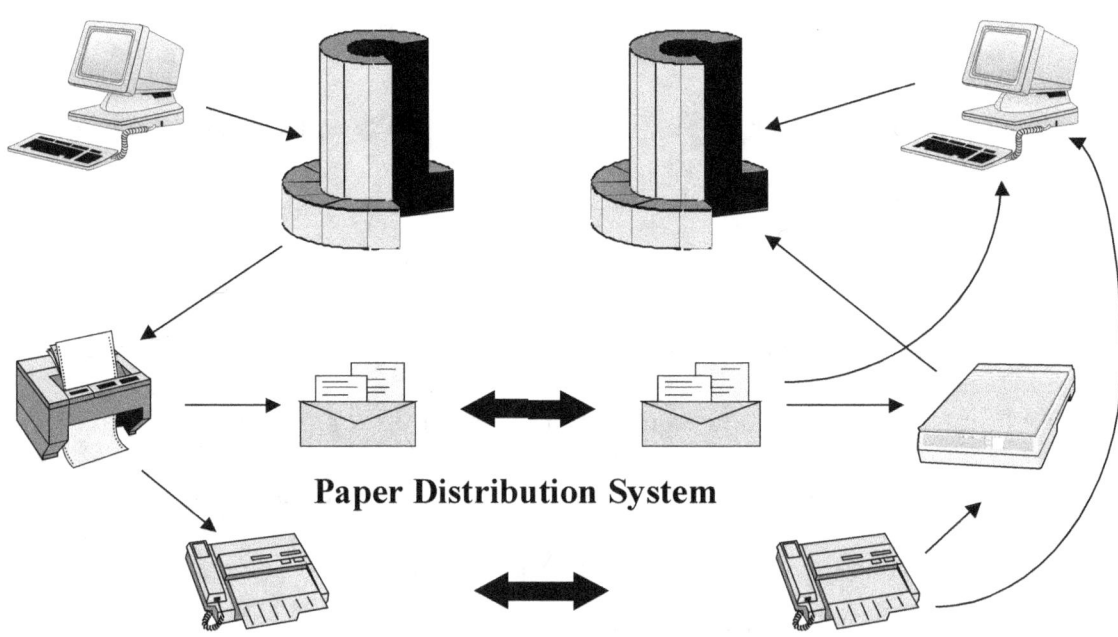

Paper Distribution System

Figure 1. Illustration of Paper Based Distribution System (Meier, 1994:10)

electronically mail the information or it must print the required data and use a manual delivery service to send the information to the receiving organization. Upon receipt of the communication, the receiving organization must manually enter the information into its own computer system if it wishes its personnel to have full information access.

Figure 2 illustrates a much more streamlined approach to the same communication procedure. Data are manually entered into the sending organization's computer system and uploaded to its central storage system. With the use of EDI, neither the sending nor the receiving organization needs to interfere with the communication process in order to affect the data transfer. EDI effectively eliminates possible error-inducing steps in the data transfer process by minimizing the requirement for human intervention.

EDI System

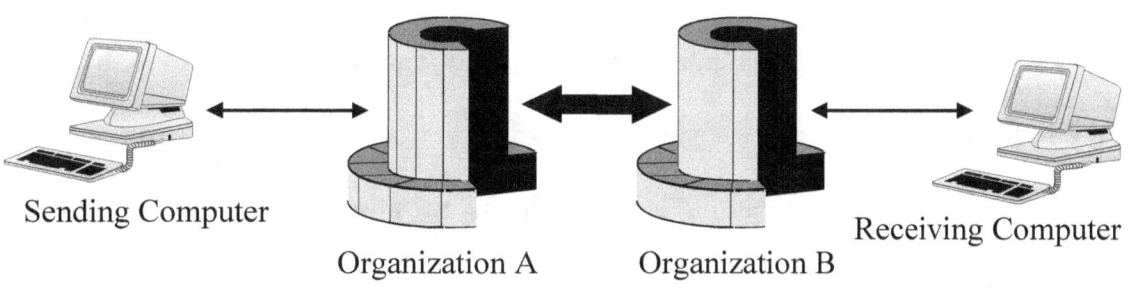

Sending Computer

Organization A Organization B

Receiving Computer

Figure 2. Illustration of EDI Based Communications System (Meier, 1996: 10)

Electronic Data Interchange Benefits. Through the elimination of the human element in the data transfer process, several benefits are realized. Meier's research identified three general benefits an organization may realize when replacing a manual data transfer system with EDI. Although different organizations will realize various levels of benefit depending on the specific use of EDI technology, most benefits will fit into one of three major categories: cost savings, data accuracy, and speed (Meier, 1994: 19).

Cost Savings. EDI provides financial savings throughout an organization. The most noticeable savings occur due to the reduction of physical documents. Costs associated with printing (printer cartridges, copying machines, paper), storage (file cabinets, file archives), and delivery (mailing and postage) are minimized. Additionally, labor costs associated with intra-organizational document handling are drastically reduced due to process automation (Meier, 1994: 20).

Data Accuracy. EDI, by its nature, improves data accuracy. The traditional data communication system is characterized by numerous data entry and re-entry operations. Each time human intervention is required to facilitate data communication, the potential for data corruption is introduced. EDI minimizes the requirement to re-enter data by transferring information from one computer system to another without human intervention, thereby reducing the possibility of costly errors (Meier, 1994: 20).

Speed. Traditional data communications systems such as the postal service and specialty courier services often require a minimum of 24 to 48 hours to transfer paper documents from one organization to another. Though this time frame can be shortened to minutes with the use of facsimile machines, or with electronic mail, the data are available only to the select few individuals to whom the correspondence was addressed. EDI reduces data transfer time to seconds, and allows for the transfer of vast quantities of data. Additionally, the computer-to-computer link provides authorized users near instantaneous access to information instead of limiting document dissemination to the addressee (Meier, 1994: 20).

Traditional data communication systems can be costly, labor intensive, prone to error, and are often slow. EDI offers a solution to each of these negative characteristics. Proper implementation of an EDI system promises improved accuracy and speed with a significant improvement in overall system data accuracy. Additionally, replacing a traditional data transfer system with an EDI system can lower long-term variable costs, thereby reducing an organizations overall operating budget (Meier, 1994: 21).

EDI Concerns. The qualities that make EDI an attractive alternative to paper-based information systems are the same qualities that provide the greatest cause for concern. Meier sums up the concerns inherent with EDI implementation:

> Although EDI has many advantages over paper-based systems care must be taken, as it must with paper documents, to ensure that EDI messages are authentic, properly authorized, and traceable. The messages also must be protected from loss, modification, or unauthorized disclosure during transmission as well as storage. (Meier, 1994: 21)

Meier divides these concerns into three general categories: auditing, legal, and security.

Auditing. Regardless of the type of information system being used, an organization must be able to check the accuracy of its processed data. Auditing gives the data credibility and enables an organization to have faith its data is correct. Regardless of which type of system (paper-based or EDI) is in place, the auditing system must accomplish the same task; the auditing system must not only verify that the data is being processed correctly, but it must also verify that the correct data are being processed (Meier, 1994: 22).

The purpose of the auditing system is to maintain control of information. Meier states, "The key to EDI auditability is having adequate controls to insure proper transaction handling. The control mechanism for an EDI system should address accuracy, completeness, security, auditability, timeliness and recoverability issues" (Meier, 1994: 22). Whether an organization uses a paper-based or an EDI based system, the requirement for auditing remains the same.

Legal. It is common practice to formally obligate oneself to the terms of a contract by the placement of a signature. The law recognizes each individual's signature as a legally binding mark on a contract. EDI transactions complicate this legal form of binding two organizations to the terms of a contract due to the absence of a verifiable, legally binding signature. Without a signature on electronic documents, the issue of contract enforceability surfaces as a serious business issue. To overcome these issues, two solutions have evolved: Trading Partner Agreements (TPA), and Electronic Signatures (Emmelhainz, 1993: 169-173).

Trading Partner Agreements (TPAs) are legally binding agreements negotiated prior to conducting business, which obligate each organization to honor the negotiated agreement terms. The TPA must be negotiated prior to conducting EDI business, and the agreement must be signed by all involved organizations (Emmelhainz, 1993: 172).

According to one expert, TPAs accomplish two primary purposes: (Meier, 1994: 24)

1. They establish the contractual relationships and references between trading partners.

2. They specify the EDI technical protocols that will be used in conducting business through EDI based transactions.

Typical areas a TPA might address include:

- Data transmittal schedules

- Procedures for resolving transaction and system errors

- Computer system back-up procedures

- Responsibilities of each partner

- Security responsibilities

The purpose of the TPA is to avoid future legal difficulties that could impact EDI transactions. By addressing each partner's concerns, a TPA helps reduce uncertainties involved with conducting EDI business by providing a legal foundation for the EDI transaction (Meier, 1994: 24).

The second area of legal concern with EDI transactions is the Electronic Signature. The signature on a contract makes the contract a valid, legally binding document. EDI transactions eliminate the physical document, and therefore leave nothing for the parties to sign. An amendment to Title 41 of the Code of Federal Regulations, Part 101-41 (41 CFR 101-41) specifically addresses the use of electronic signatures in the execution of EDI transactions (Meier, 1994: 25). This regulation reads:

> Electronic Data Interchange (EDI) means the electronic exchange of transportation information by means of electronic transmission of the information in lieu of the creation of a paper document....[A] signature, in the case of an EDI transmission, means a discreet authenticating code intended to bind parties to the terms and conditions of a contract. (Title 41, 1992)

Trading partners need only establish a system of electronic authentication, and both organizations can legally enter into a contract without signing a physical document.

Security. The issue of system security is the final major concern with EDI transactions. Information security is a major concern for most large organizations. Most organizations would agree information security is not a luxury, but a necessity in today's highly competitive market. A business can lose its edge in the market if competitors are able to intercept information integral to business operations. Even if an EDI system offers tremendous cost savings and a distinct competitive advantage, it must also provide adequate levels of secure communications capability. If security needs cannot be met, the advantages associated with EDI implementation may be outweighed by the risk of information piracy.

In June 1991, the National Institute of Standards and Technology addressed concerns associated with EDI security by publishing a Computer Systems Laboratory (CSL) Bulletin on computer systems technology (Meier, 1994: 25). The CSL Bulletin established general guidelines to address EDI security concerns: (Hardcastle, 1992: 5-2 – 5-3)

- Message Integrity: The transmitting activity must ensure that all critical information transmitted is received unchanged.

- Confidentiality: Activities must restrict access to EDI transactions that contain personal, trade-secret, or sensitive data.

- Originator Authentication: The receiving activity must have assurance that the EDI message was transmitted by the indicated originator.

- Nonrepudiation: Those activities establishing EDI systems must ensure that binding proposals submitted by any of the trading partners cannot be denied.

- Availability: All activities must develop back-up procedures for the protection of important data in case of systems failure.

Electronic Data Interchange is a natural progression of communications technology. The proliferation of inexpensive high-speed computer systems provides an economical means for almost any organization to drastically reduce its dependence on paper-based communications systems. Although the fixed costs associated with developing a computer network may be high, the low variable costs associated with its operation make EDI systems cost effective, long-term alternatives to traditional paper-based communications.

Due to the many possible applications of EDI technology and the potential benefits of its application, there has been a dramatic increase in EDI use (Lambert, 1993: 534). As stated by one expert: "The global information economy of the future will rest on a global network and EDI will be behind this" (Naisbitt, 1988: 3). Transportation was one of the first industries to realize and seize upon the benefits of EDI technology. Lambert illustrates the proliferation of EDI technology throughout the transportation industry with these examples: (Lambert, 1993: 535)

- Union Pacific conducts 80 percent of its interline transactions electronically.

- Carolina Freight Carriers transmits approximately 1,200 customer invoices electronically each week.

- Over 70 percent of the interline waybill traffic on 13 railroads is handled electronically.

- Railing Corporation, an Association of American Railroads subsidiary, has a computer database that contains the railroad industry's entire inventory of railcars, containers, and trailers; it receives electronic reports of over 60 percent of car movements in the United States.

- A customer of Roadway Express has eliminated all paper flow between itself and the motor carrier. Roadway receives payments from the customer electronically, based on direct data transmissions.

With the commercial sector adopting EDI technology as the industry standard, the DoD has no choice but to take note. With an increased dependence upon commercial transportation, the DoD must modernize the DTS and establish a common communications capability with its civilian trading partners. USTRANSCOMs first step in establishing this integral communications link between the DoD and commercial carriers is the development of an internal electronic tracking system. Once established, this system will provide the ITV so desperately needed by field commanders.

In-transit Visibility

Following Desert Storm, the Deputy Under Secretary of Defense (Logistics), established the requirement for the DoD to develop a system which could maintain visibility of all assets, this concept was known as Total Asset Visibility (TAV). The *Defense In-transit Visibility Integration Plan* defines TAV as "the capability that permits operational and logistics managers to determine and act on timely and accurate information about the location, quantity, condition, movement, and status of Defense materiel" (DoD, 1997: B-3). Figure 3 illustrates the concept of Total Asset Visibility as an integration of three key components: (DoD, 1997: 1-7)

1. In-Process Visibility- tracking assets in various stages of procurement or repair.

2. In-Storage Visibility- tracking assets being stored (inventory at Defense storage locations).

3. In-Transit Visibility- tracking assets within the DTS.

17

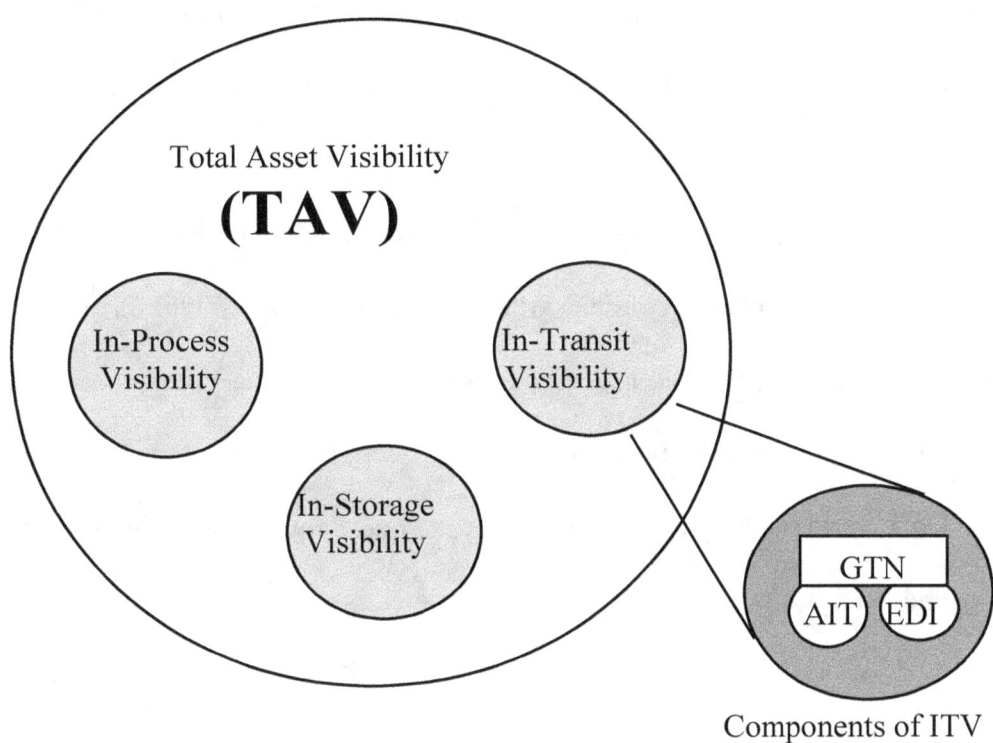

Figure 3. Total Asset Visibility and It's Three Key Components (Wolford, 1996: 7)

Although all three components are required to provide TAV, this paper is only concerned with ITV and how this fits into the greater vision of DoD leaders. The *Defense In-transit Visibility Plan* defines ITV as

> The ability to track the identity, status, and location of DoD unit and non-unit cargo (excluding bulk petroleum, oils, and lubricants); passengers; medical patients; and personal property from origin to the consignee or destination designated by the CINCs, Military Services, or Defense agencies, during peace, contingencies, and war.

Providing ITV is not an easy task. The DoD has long been challenged with the problem of keeping track of its assets and personnel. Commercial transportation companies such as Emery, United Parcel Service (UPS), and Federal Express (FedEx) pride themselves on their ability to provide customers with near-instantaneous access to shipment information 24 hours a day, 7 days a week (Wolford, 1996: 5). The ability to track packages throughout their transportation network and provide customers visibility of a packages whereabouts is a key service (or core competency), integral to the success of these companies.

Following Desert Storm, the DoD realized it could no longer use "brute force logistics" if it expected to continue winning wars (Wolford, 1996: 1). The DoD realized, much like Emery, UPS, and FedEx, that if it expected to meet the needs of its customers, it would have to improve the efficiency and effectiveness of its transportation system. The DoD could no longer afford to lose or misplace equipment. The primary problem with the DTS, from a field commander's perspective, was an inability to determine the status of equipment that had been ordered. Without the ability to determine the status of equipment in the DTS pipeline, commanders would order the same piece of equipment several times assuming the original order had been lost, stolen, or possibly never even received. The reality was that equipment was slow to arrive because of an overburdened transportation system; much of the burden created by the transportation of multiple pieces of equipment meant to satisfy a single order. As stated earlier, the net effect of commanders reordering equipment time and time again combined with inadequate visibility was more than 20,000 of 40,000 containers entering the theater had to be stopped, opened, inventoried, resealed, and reentered into the transportation system. The effect of these inefficiencies was the unnecessary delay of time-sensitive cargo to the soldier in the field, and an estimated $150 million paid for the storage and detention of cargo containers (DoD, 1995a: 1-1).

Global Transportation Network. The Global Transportation Network (GTN) is the backbone of USTRANSCOM's ITV initiative. To provide millions of soldiers, airmen, sailors, and marines visibility of their equipment while it is in the DTS pipeline, USTRANSCOM developed the Global Transportation Network. Following Desert Shield/Desert Storm, General Hansford T. Johnson, Commander in Chief, USTRANSCOM, September 1989-August 1992, outlined his concept of GTN and its relationship to the Joint Operation Planning and Execution System (JOPES):

> Ultimately, the Global Transportation Network will be the automated data processing system for US Transportation Command. We will still have something like JOPES…for various operation plans. But you have to have a way of communicating the transportation requirement from JOPES to the mode operator. Then you have to follow the shipment, advise a customer when it is arriving, and provide feedback. GTN will do that. But in doing so, it will allow us to have total asset visibility, at least for the time the cargo is in the transportation system. It allows us to execute our missions with better, more timely information. It allows everybody in the system to know the same thing at the same time. (Matthews, 1996: 26)

The purpose of the GTN was to eliminate the most common complaint by DTS users during and after Desert Storm—the lack of ITV (Matthews, 1996: 26). According to Matthews, "with the capability to identify and track cargo and passengers en route, from origin to final destination, ITV offered tremendous benefits to warfighters" (Matthews, 1996: 27). With ITV, the warfighter was able to get real-time verification of cargo locations preventing unnecessary reordering of equipment. "Consequently, scarce lift resources would be freed to carry truly critical cargo" (Matthews, 1996: 27).

The challenge of the GTN implementation is gathering and integrating information from numerous diverse data sources to provide a single overarching data repository. Prior to the GTN, each government agency using the DTS had its own system for tracking intransit cargo. As a result of this fragmentation, the GTN architecture is a complex splicing of over 25 different computer systems and networks. Table 1 shows all

20

computer systems interfacing with the GTN as of April 1999. An explanation of each

system is provided in Appendix A.

Table 1. Systems Interfacing With The Global Transportation Network
(USTRANSCOM, 1999: 65-6)

System	Owner	Class	Locations	Direction of Interface	GTN Version	
					Current	FOC[1]
GCCS	JCS	S	CINC's Headquarters, NMCC, Service Headquarters, and other defense Agency Headquarters.	To GTN From GTN	X	
JOPES	JCS	S	CINC's Headquarters, NMCC, Service Headquarters, and other defense Agency Headquarters.	To GTN From GTN	X	
DAASC	DLA	U, S	DAASC, Wright Patterson AFB, OH DAASC, Tracy, CA	To GTN From GTN	X X	ESI[2] ESI
GDSS	AMC	U	Scott AFB, IL Travis AFB, CA (Alt Site)	To GTN	X	ESI
GATES	AMC	U	Scott AFB, IL	To GTN		ESI
CAPS II	AMC	U	Aerial Ports Worldwide	To GTN	X	
IBS	MTMC	U	MTMC-EA, Bayonne, NJ MTMC-WA, Oakland, CA	To GTN		ESI ESI
WPS	MTMC	U	MTMC-EA, Bayonne, NJ MTMC-WA, Oakland, CA Ports Worldwide	To GTN	X X X	
DTTS	US Navy	U	Navy Base, Norfolk, VA	To GTN	X	
CFM	MTMC	U	MTMC, Falls Church, VA	To GTN	X	
TCAIMS II	US Army	U	Army installations, bases, and stations	To GTN		ESI
TC ACCIS	US Army	U	Army installations, bases, and stations	To GTN	X	
CMOS	USAF	U	USAF Standard System Center Maxwell AFB, Montgomery, AL	To GTN	X	ESI
TRAC2ES	USTC	U	Multiple Installations	To GTN From GTN		
IC3	MSC	S	Navy Yard, Wash, DC	To GTN	X	ESI
AMS	MTMC	U	MTMC, Falls Church, VA	To GTN	X	Y2K[3]
BROKER	AMC	U	Scott AFB, IL	To GTN	X	
ADANS	AMC	U, S	Scott AFB, IL	To GTN	X	
JALIS	US Navy	U	New Orleans, LA	To GTN	X	ESI

Table 1. (Continued)

System	Owner	Class	Locations	Direction of Interface	GTN Version Current	FOC[1]
GOPAX	MTMC	U	MTMC, Falls Church, VA	To GTN	X	IGTN[4]
CEDI VAN/TPS	CSX	U	CSX, Jacksonville, FL	To GTN	X	CEDI[5]
JTAV	DoD	U	Worldwide Locations	From GTN	X	
SALTS	US Navy	U	Worldwide Locations	From GTN	X	
LIA Regional servers	US Army	U	Fredricksfeld, Germany	To GTN		ESI
DTTS-E	DoD	U	Fredricksfeld, Germany	To GTN	X	ESI

[1] Future Operational Concept
[2] External System Interface Project
[3] Year 2000 Project
[4] Interactive GTN Project
[5] Commercial Electronic Data Interchange Project

It is interesting to note that even within one particular agency, numerous computer systems are used to maintain visibility over cargo and personnel movements. The variety of each service's mission requirements and operational environments mandate the use of several systems, each with unique capabilities. Figure 4 illustrates the diverse range of customers currently using GTN to facilitate ITV (USTRANSCOM, 1999: 50).

The GTN is a complex computer network designed to meet the ITV needs of thousands of DTS customers. To be effective, the GTN must be able to communicate simultaneously with numerous computer systems worldwide. In addition, the GTN must be able to provide each user accurate up-to-date information on cargo and personnel movements.

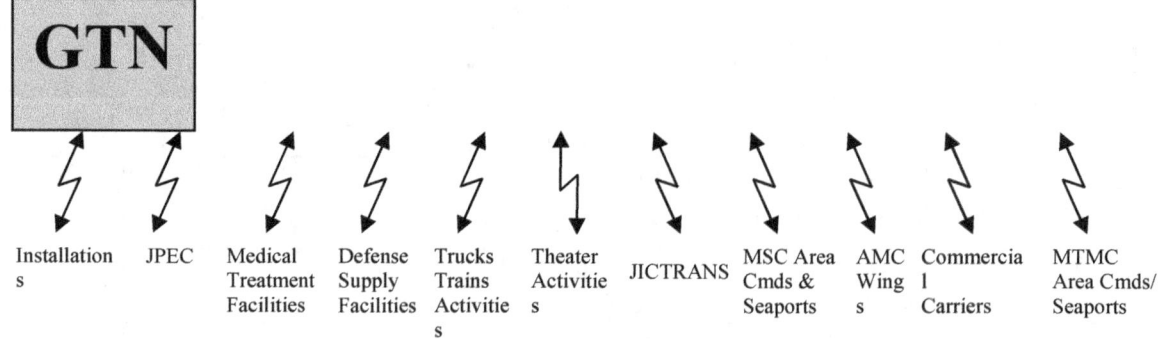

Figure 4: Current GTN Users (USTRANSCOM, 1999: 50)

Chapter Summary

The lack of ITV is a long-standing problem in the Defense Transportation System. With declining defense budgets and the shift in our nation's National Defense Strategy, the Department of Defense was forced to explore alternatives that improve operational efficiency and effectiveness within the Defense Transportation System.

To facilitate ITV and ultimately TAV, USTRANSCOM designed the Global Transportation Network. The GTN is designed to link all government agencies conducting business within the DTS and provide a common database of movement information. For GTN to be effective, it must provide each user accurate information on all shipments of interest regardless of the shipments origin. Data from all sources to include military, DoD, and commercial must be available if the GTN is to be considered successful in its primary mission of establishing ITV.

III. Establishing an EDI Need

Introduction

Thus far, this paper has been concerned with establishing a basic working knowledge of the DTS and DoD ITV objectives. It is now time to investigate the DoD's requirement for EDI. Desert Storm highlighted the US Armed Forces dependency on commercial transportation assets. Without Civil Reserve Air Fleet (CRAF) activation, and an ability to greatly augment US sealift capabilities, US Forces would have experienced difficulty assembling and sustaining the dominant fighting force that invaded Iraq on 23 February 1991. Since the culmination of Desert Storm, the DoD has further reduced its personnel and transportation assets exacerbating its reliance on commercial carriers. This chapter quantifies US military dependence upon commercial carriers and establishes DoD's requirement for a commercial carrier EDI interface.

Desert Storm Civilian Involvement

The Desert Shield/Desert Storm mobilization ranks as one of the largest deployments in US history. During the eight months comprising the operation, which began on 7 August 1990 and ended 10 March 1991 (beginning of redeployment), USTRANSCOM "moved to USCENTCOM's area of responsibility nearly 504,000 passengers, 3.6 million tons of dry cargo, and 6.1 million tons of petroleum products" (Matthews, 1996: 12). In comparison, "during the first three weeks of Desert Shield,

USTRANSCOM moved more passengers and equipment to the Persian Gulf than the United States transported to Korea during the first three months of the Korean War" (Matthews, 1996: 12).

The successful deployment of troops and equipment was key to US success in the Persian Gulf, and could not have been accomplished without the assistance of commercial carriers.

The data in Table 2 show the amount of personnel and cargo transported via airlift during Operations Desert Shield and Desert Storm. Overall, commercial carriers flew more than 20 percent of all missions and carried nearly 65 percent of all passengers and almost 30 percent of all cargo short tons during Persian Gulf operations.

Table 2. Desert Shield/Desert Storm Strategic Airlift Totals
(Matthews, 1996: 39-40)
(August 1990 to 10 March 1991)

Aircraft Type	Missions		Passengers		Cargo (Short Tons)	
	Number	% of Total	Number	% of Total	Number	% of Total
C-141	8,536	52.68%	93,126	18.64%	159,462	30.30%
C-5	3,770	23.27%	84,385	16.89%	201,685	38.32%
C-9	209	1.29%	0	0.00%	0	0.00%
KC-10	379	2.34%	1,111	0.22%	19,905	3.78%
Commercial	3,309	20.42%	321,005	64.25%	145,225	27.59%
TOTAL	**16,203**		**499,627**		**526,277**	

In addition to the amount of cargo and personnel transported, commercial carriers also provided a great deal of asset flexibility for airlift planners. For example, a Boeing 747 can carry about the same number of passengers as a C-5. But when a 747 is chartered to carry the passengers, the C-5 can now either carry more passengers or it can haul outsized cargo which will not fit on any other aircraft.

The DoD also gained considerable capability from commercial sealift during Operations Desert Shield and Desert Storm. Table 3 shows all unit equipment transported by sealift (due to data limitations, ammunition shipments are not included in totals). The data show over 56 percent of all shiploads and nearly 40 percent of all cargo short tons were delivered to the AOR by a commercial source.

Table 3. Desert Shield/Storm Strategic Sealift Of Unit Equipment By Shipping Source (Matthews, 1996: 116)
(August 1990 to 10 March 1991)

	Ship Loads		Cargo (Short Tons)	
Type of Ship	# Loads	% of Total	# ST	% of Total
Fast Sealift Ships	32	6.97%	321,941	13.24%
Prepositioning Ships	20	4.36%	206,836	8.51%
Maritime Prepositioning Ships	26	5.66%	257,444	10.59%
Ready Reserve Force	123	26.80%	691,048	28.42%
US Flag Commercial	62	13.51%	308,285	12.68%
Foreign Flag Commercial	196	42.70%	646,315	26.58%
Military Total	201	43.79%	1,477,269	60.75%
Commercial Total	258	56.21%	954,600	39.25%
Total	459		2,431,869	

It cannot be said that Operation Desert Storm would have failed without commercial transportation carriers; but commercial carriers provided US forces a distinct strategic advantage. Without commercial carrier involvement, the United States would never have massed the invading force that attacked Saddam Hussein's Republican Guard on 23 February 1991.

United States Military Downsizing

Following Desert Storm, the US Military was riding high on its victory over Iraq. And, as has happened after every major conflict, the United States began a major reduction in military force capability. During the past 10 years since Desert Storm, the DoD has been reduced in every imaginable way. The data in Table 4 show the reduction of DoD personnel during the period of 1990 to 2000. In addition to personnel reductions, the Air Force has had major reductions in its strategic airlift force. Table 5 shows the reduction in available aircraft from 1990 to 1999. According to the DoD *Strategic Objective Plan*, in addition to the force reductions, "the overall defense budget has declined 28 percent in constant dollars; and funds to procure new weapons have dropped 50 percent. By contrast, the number of troop deployments over the last 12 years has increased about 160 percent, from 26 to 68 annually" (GAO, 2000: 3).

Table 4. DoD Personnel Reductions From 1990 to 2000
(Jones, 2000)

	Personnel (Thousands)		
	1990	2000	Reduction
Active Duty Military	2,069	1,384	-33%
Reserve Military	1,170	865	-26%
DoD Civilian	1,107	700	-37%

The combination of fewer assets and increased operational tempo forced the DoD to look outside the confines of its own resources and procure alternate methods of transporting its assets in time of conflict or humanitarian operation. Recent operations highlight the DoDs' increased dependence upon commercial carriers. The data presented in Table 6 summarize airlift operations in support of Kosovo humanitarian efforts.

Table 5. Airlift Asset Comparison 1990 to 1999
*(Matthews, 1996: 15)
**(HQ AMC, 1999: 80)

	Strategic Aircraft		
Type Aircraft	1990*	1999**	Change
C-141B	234	121	-113
C-5A/B	110	104	-6
C-17A	0	37	37
KC-10A	59	59	0
TOTAL	403	321	-82

Although this is a much smaller operation than Operation Desert Shield/Storm, this effort highlights a growing trend in the DoD, reliance upon commercial carriers to fill transportation needs. During Kosovo humanitarian efforts, over 85 percent of all airlift missions and nearly 92 percent of all cargo (by weight) was transported by chartered civilian airlift.

Reliance upon the commercial sector for our nations defense transportation requirements is a trend established during Operation Desert Storm and one that continues today. Even when US forces are not committed to hostile or humanitarian operations, the DoD is incapable of meeting the transportation needs of its commanders. According to one expert, 80 percent of all peacetime DoD cargo is transported via the commercial sector (MacKeen, 1999). DoD commercial carriers are as much a part of the DTS system as any DoD owned aircraft, ship or truck.

Table 6. Kosovo Humanitarian Airlift In Support of Operation Allied Force
03 April – 18 May 1999
(HQ AMC TACC/XOO, 1999)

Aircraft Type	Missions Number	% of Total	Passengers Number	% of Total	Cargo (Short Tons) Number	% of Total
Military Airlift						
C-5	2	4.26%		0%	165	4.36%
C-17	4	8.51%	50	98%	152	4.02%
C-130	1	2.13%	1	2%	12.5	0.33%
Total	7	14.89%	51	100%	329.5	8.71%
Commercial Airlift						
B-747	37	78.72%			3243.2	85.74%
MD-11	2	4.26%			170	4.49%
DC-8	1	2.13%			40	1.06%
Total	40	85.11%			3453.2	91.29%
TOTAL	47		51		3782.7	

The EDI Requirement

There are two main reasons the DoD must invest its limited resources and establish an EDI connection with the commercial sector. First, in-transit visibility means visibility of everything, not just cargo and personnel transported through organic means. Second, the largest carriers in the commercial sector have already committed to EDI as the preferred way of doing business, and they want their business partners to develop compatible EDI capabilities.

ITV Requirement. In 1994, the DoD developed its initial plan for achieving ITV of all DoD shipments, unit equipment, and personnel moving throughout the DTS (DoD, 1996: 3-7). As the volume of equipment and personnel being tracked by the GTN increased, efforts to automate data entry were accelerated. In a letter dated 13 August

1999, General Charles T. Robertson, Commander in Chief, USTRANSCOM stated, "The real catalyst in the military affairs revolution is the ability to manage vast amounts of information across all spectrums. Our ultimate solution for managing information is by using the above tools [EDI principles and technologies]" (Robertson, 1999).

Commercial Carriers. Commercial carriers, like all businesses operate with tight profit margins. As has already been stated, EDI has numerous business advantages to include cost savings, data accuracy, and increased communications speed. Once a company has invested in an EDI system, it can only reap full benefits if all its customers use EDI technology. If customers must operate within the confines of a paper-based communications system, then a company attempting to exploit EDI capabilities will be required to maintain infrastructure to support both a paper-based and an EDI-based system. Therefore, the commercial sector wants the DoD to develop a compatible EDI capability.

Chapter Summary

The DoD has a genuine operational requirement for EDI. The military services needed commercial sector augmentation during Desert Storm in order to move the vast quantities of troops and equipment required of the invasion. Since Desert Storm, the military force has shrunk by over 30 percent contributing to the DoD dependence upon commercial carriers for all transportation requirements. But, with more cargo moving by commercial means, the DoD has a tough job maintaining ITV of all its assets.

EDI offers a solution to the DoD. EDI technology can provide a means for the DoD to continue to receive shipment status reports on its valuable equipment. Not only does EDI provide a way for the DoD to continue to have ITV of its in-transit assets, but it is also the preferred method of conducting business with most transportation companies.

IV. The DoD EDI System

Introduction

On January 18, 1995, the Deputy Under Secretary of Defense for Logistics (DUSD(L)) designated USTRANSCOM as lead agent to accelerate implementation of electronic data interchange in the Defense Transportation System (Barkley, 1997). Initial EDI efforts focused on electronic rate tenders, government bills of lading, and fund transfers. As the program matured, the DoD recognized the value of EDI to ITV initiatives and planned to have interface capability between GTN and commercial carriers by mid 1996. This chapter discusses the Defense Transportation EDI Integration Plan and USTRANSCOM's vision for developing an electronic commerce capability that simultaneously provides source data for ITV purposes.

Defense Transportation EDI Process

Every activity involved in moving cargo and personnel through the DTS requires some level of information concerning the shipment. To enhance the marriage between EDI and the DTS, USTRANSCOM established the *Defense Transportation EDI (DTEDI) Program Integration Plan.* The plan divides the Defense transportation freight movement process into 11 activities with each falling into one of four areas: tender submission, planning, movement, and payment (DoD, 1996: 3-1). Figure 5 depicts the DoD

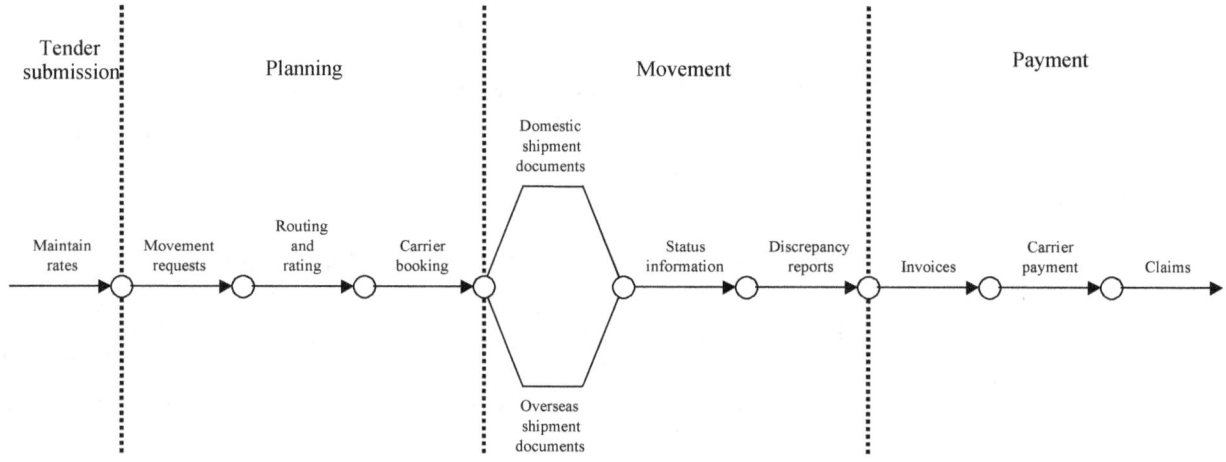

Figure 5. Defense Transportation EDI Processes (DoD, 1996: 3-1)

Transportation Processes as illustrated in the *Defense EDI Program Implementation Plan*. Figure 6 demonstrates how the four areas of the transportation EDI process work to provide ITV from beginning to end. MTMC's CONUS Freight Management (CFM) System will provide DTEDI freight payment shipment information to GTN for ITV applications.

Tender Submission. Before scheduling a cargo shipment, the intended shipper must have access to carrier rate information. Tender submission consists of only one action, maintaining rate information. The plan calls for automation of the rate filing process in each of three areas: guaranteed traffic (GT), voluntary/negotiated tenders, and overseas rate agreements (DoD, 1996: C-2). "When fully implemented, Military Traffic Management Command's (MTMC) EDI systems will enable it to receive and store transportation rates electronically for retrieval by shippers during the routing and rating process" (DoD, 1996: 3-2).

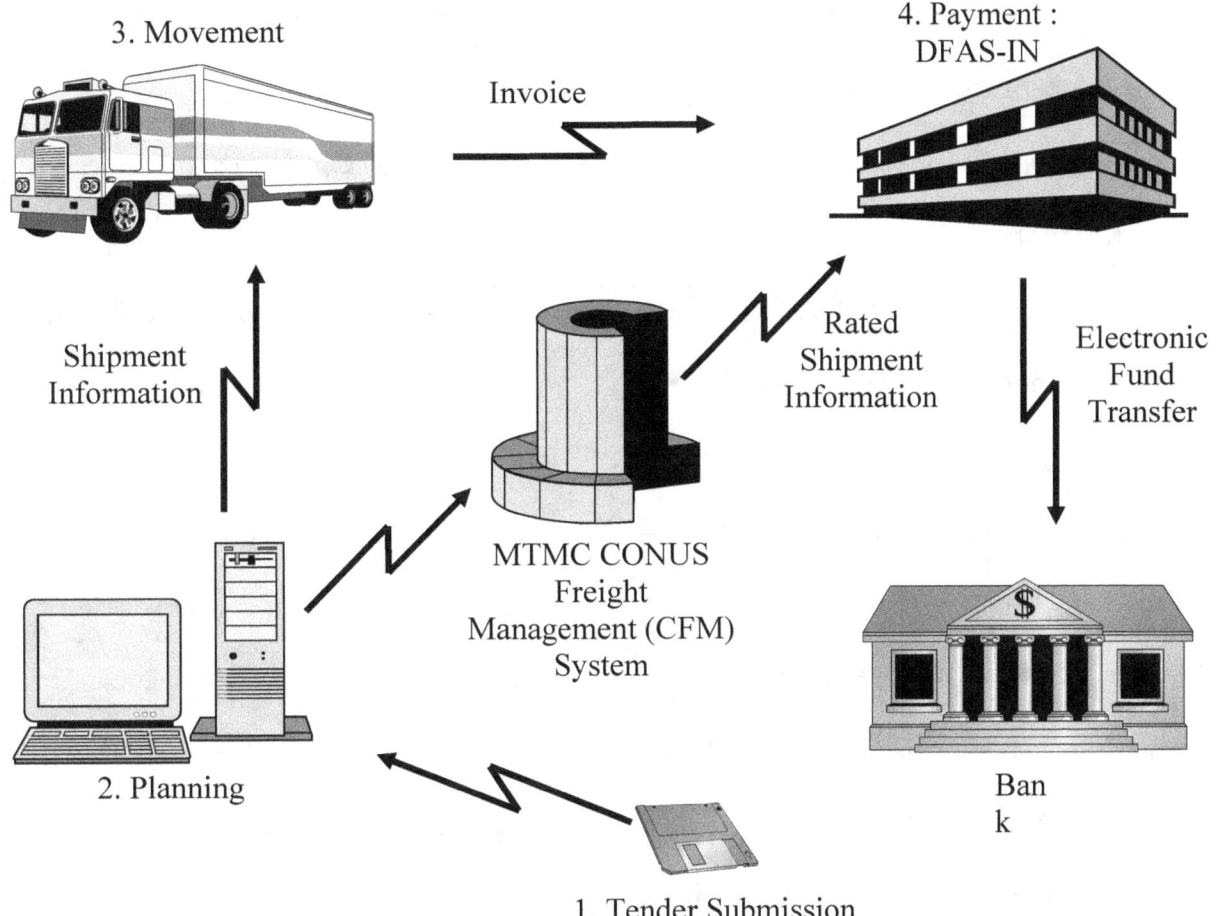

3. Movement

4. Payment :
DFAS-IN

Invoice

Shipment
Information

Rated
Shipment
Information

Electronic
Fund
Transfer

MTMC CONUS
Freight
Management (CFM)
System

2. Planning

Ban
k

1. Tender Submission

Figure 6. DTEDI Operating Concept (DoD, 1997: 1-6)

Planning. The transportation planning area consists of three processes:

movement requests, routing and rating, and carrier booking.

Movement Requests. Most agencies initiate the movement of cargo or

personnel with a movement request submitted to the installation transportation officer.

The transportation officer then enters the requested shipment into a planning system.

Once the information is entered, the system combines shipments by mode and destination.

Routing and Rates. Once the movement of material has been planned, the shipper then submits an electronic routing request to MTMC. In return, MTMC sends the shipper a list of potential carriers and their rates. Upon receipt, the shipper selects a carrier for booking (Wolford, 1996: 26).

Carrier Booking. "Except for a carrier booking prototype that MTMC developed for its Integrated Booking System, no other shipper or port system incorporates an electronic booking capability" (DoD, 1996: C-10). Most shippers continue to use telephone and facsimile equipment to maintain close contact with their carriers. But the current trend indicates commercial carriers are more regularly using their own form of EDI transactions to schedule appointments, book freight, and confirm and cancel bookings (DoD, 1996: 3-3).

Movement. The movement area consists of four processes: domestic shipment documents, overseas shipment documents, status information, and discrepancy reports (DoD, 1996: 3-3).

Domestic Shipment Documents. The Domestic Shipment documents are divided into two categories: bills of lading from the shipper to the finance center and bill of lading from the shipper to the carrier, consignees, and others involved (DoD, 1996: C-12).

The DTEDI system must be capable of electronically processing Government Bills of Lading (GBLs), Commercial Bills of Lading (CBLs), and other essential commercial information. Additionally, the DTEDI system must be able to transfer bill of

35

lading information with Defense Finance and Accounting System-Indianapolis (DFAS-IN), General Services Administration (GSA), MTMC, consignees, and the commercial carriers in order to support the GBL payment program. In support of the DoD's ITV program, shipment information must also be transmitted to USTRANSCOM's GTN.

Overseas Shipment Documents. Shippers use various documents, including GBLs, Transportation Control and Movement Documents (TCMDs), and commercial specific documents to move shipments to ports of embarkation (POEs). However, POEs lack the capability to receive or create TCMDs and manifests using commercially accepted standards (DoD, 1996: 3-4). Additionally, many foreign carriers lack an EDI capability due to the high cost associated with start-up and the technology required to establish an effective EDI system. This complex problem presents a major challenge for worldwide EDI use in the DTS (Wolford, 1996: 29).

Status Information. For the ITV program to succeed, each node of the DTS must be capable of generating detailed shipment status reports and must forward this information to the GTN (DoD, 1996: C-22).

Discrepancy Reports. All nodes of the DTS must have the capability to generate a discrepancy report when the contents, description, or condition of the cargo do not match the associated shipment. This type of information is used to file financial claims with carriers for lost or damaged items (DoD, 1996: C-24).

Payment. The payment area is divided into three separate areas: invoices, carrier payment, and claims (DoD, 1996: 3-5).

Invoices. DFAS uses the Defense Transportation Payment System (DTRS) to electronically collect invoice and shipment information from commercial carriers. The Defense transportation community is focusing on increasing the number of EDI-capable carriers in order to take full advantage of efficient business practices (DoD, 1996: 3-5).

Carrier Payment. DoD benefits in two ways by automating carrier payments – it avoids the cost of writing and distributing checks, and it frees personnel positions for other responsibilities (DoD, 1996: C-28). This operating concept calls for DFAS-IN's DTRS to furnish invoice data need to affect the electronic fund transfer (EFT). Unlike other EDI transactions, the EFT not only requires cooperation between the DoD and a commercial carrier, it also requires the cooperation of a bank to complete the transaction (Wolford, 1996: 30).

Claims. The final step in the Defense transportation process is making a claim for lost or damaged shipments. It is estimated that the DFAS-IN receives approximately 15,000 claims annually (DoD, 1996: C-30). Once it is determined that the shipper has a legitimate claim against a carrier, EDI can be used to send a request for payment.

The initial focus of the DTEDI program is to support initiatives that reduce the amount of human labor required to process equipment for commercial carrier shipment. The four process areas that make up the Defense transportation system--tender submission, planning, movement, and payment--remained unchanged, whether the DTS is operated using a paper-based or EDI-based system. But with commercial carriers adopting EDI as the standard way of conducting business, USTRANSCOM, through implementation of the DTEDI Integration Plan, has designed a system to support electronic audit and payment of freight and personal property shipment invoices.

Additionally, the DTEDI program establishes the infrastructure that allows USTRANSCOM to capture valuable source data for ITV purposes (Wolford, 1996: 31).

EDI Transaction Set Standards

The success of the DTEDI ITV effort is contingent upon the ability of GTN to effectively communicate with DoD trading partner computer systems. For two computer systems to communicate, the transmitted data must be formatted to an agreed upon standard. The use of standards is critical to EDI and is key to making EDI a practical way of doing business. According to one expert, there are two ideas that must be kept in mind when discussing standards:

- Compliance with the standards is voluntary (Meier, 1994: 28). The use of a particular standard will normally be set forth in a TPA.

- The standards specify only the format, rules, and data content of electronic business transactions, they do not address how trading partners will establish the required physical communications link to exchange the EDI data (Meier, 1994: 28).

Types of Data Format Standards. Several types of EDI standards have been developed to ease communications between organizations. These different standards can normally be classified into one of four categories: (Hinge, 1988: 22)

- Proprietary. Proprietary data standards are those established by individual organizations for communicating with trading partners within a closed system.

- Industry-Specific. While proprietary data standards are established by individual organizations, industry-specific standards are set by an industry trade group to promote intra-industry electronic communication.

- Cross-Industry. In the United States there is only one inter-industry EDI data format: the American National Standards Institute (ANSI) Accredited Standard Committee X12 (ASC X12) standard.

- International. While ASC X12 is the standard for EDI in the US, the standard for use in Europe and in many other parts of the world is the United Nations/EDI for Administration, Commerce, and Transport (EDIFACT).

When deciding upon a data standard, USTRANSCOM had to consider the global nature of the DTS operation. Obviously, the proprietary and industry-specific standards would accommodate only a select group of trading partners. Because the DTS is continuously adding and deleting business partners, neither of these types of standards would be appropriate for the DTS. USTRANSCOM decided to adopt the cross-industry standard established by the ANSI. Table 7 shows a list of transaction types supported by the ANSI ASC X12 standard.

Table 7. ASC X12 Transaction Sets
(Frohman, 1998: A-2)

Set Number	Transaction Set Name	Reference Number
110	Air Freight Details and Invoice	X12.100
204	Motor Carrier Shipment Information	X12.103
210	Motor Carrier Freight Details and Invoice	X12.104
213	Motor Carrier Shipment Status Inquiry	X12.105
214	Transportation Carrier Shipment Status Message	X12.106
300	Reservation (Booking Request) (Ocean)	X12.109
301	Confirmation (Ocean)	X12.109
303	Booking Cancellation (Ocean)	X12.110
304	Shipping Instructions	X12.113
309	U.S. Customs Manifest (Ocean)	X12.117
310	Freight Receipt and Invoice (Ocean)	X12.118
312	Arrival Notice (Ocean)	X12.119
315	Status Details (Ocean)	X12.122
353	U.S. Customs Events Advisory Details	X12.132
355	U.S. Customs Manifest Rejection	X12.134
410	Rail Carrier Freight Details and Invoice	X12.139
421	Estimated Time of Arrival and Car Scheduling	X12.261

Table 7. (Continued)

Set Number	Transaction Set Name	Reference Number
422	Shipper's Car Order	X12.262
511	Requisition	X12.225
602	Transportation Services Tender	X12.126
820	Payment Order Remittance Advice	X12.4
824	Application Advice	X12.44
842	Nonconformance Report	X12.21
850	Purchase Order	X12.1
856	Ship Notice/Manifest	X12.10
858	Shipment Information	X12.18
859	Freight Invoice	X12.55
864	Text Message	X12.34
867	Product Transfer and Resale Report	X12.33
920	Loss or Damage Claim--General Commodities	X12.174
925	Claim Tracer	X12.176
926	Claim Status Report and Tracer Reply	X12.177
940	Warehouse Shipping Order	X12.189
945	Warehouse Shipping Advice	X12.194
990	Response to a Load Tender	X12.180

At first inspection it may be of concern that the international standard EDIFACT was not selected as the standard for a global transportation system. But, when USTRANSCOM made the decision to adopt the ANSI standard, ANSI's ASC X12 standard was the predominant EDI standard in the US. Also, in 1995 a task force was charged to make ASC X12 and EDIFACT compatible. Since 1997, there have been no new ASC X12 specific data sets developed (Sutton, 1997: 11). The result is that USTRANSCOM indirectly adopted a universally accepted EDI standard.

EDI Data Capturing

USTRANSCOM had several options available when deciding how best to capture EDI data. The challenge was how best to interface with trading partners. Established companies like FedEx, UPS, and J.B. Hunt have had EDI systems for many years. Not only is USTRANSCOM's GTN not compatible with the X12 data standard, but also many companies with established systems chose proprietary or industry-standards as their preferred method of conducting EDI transactions and therefore are also incompatible with X12 standards. USTRANSCOM was forced to solve its data incompatibility problem or it would not have an adequate EDI system.

To fix the data incompatibility problem, USTRANSCOM needed a way to decode incoming data to a form accepted by GTN. USTRANSCOM finally settled on an EDI architecture that used a value added network or VAN as a go-between the DoD and commercial trading partners.

Required EDI VAN Services. Because the VAN is integral to DoD operations, the VAN must meet stringent standards of operation. The DTEDI program classifies required VAN services into seven categories: data processing; transmission, access, and protocol; security; survivability; operational facilities; report facilities; and customer support.

Data Processing. The VAN must have the ability to electronically store, retrieve, and forward EDI business documents for trading partners in electronic mailboxes located on a host computer. The VAN must also be capable of converting ASC X12; Transportation Data Coordinating Committee (TDCC); Uniform Communications Standard (UCS); and EDIFACT encoded EDI transactions into non-EDI formats which can then be transmitted to facsimile machines, printers, or via email (DoD, 1996: B-1).

Transmission, Access, and Protocol. The EDI VAN is the information pipeline connecting the DTS to commercial trading partners, and therefore must provide transparent, reliable service. According to the *DTEDI Program Implementation Plan*, to be effective the VAN must provide the following services: (DoD, 1996: B-2)

- Third party interconnection. A network interconnection acknowledgment that is sent when data are sent to or received from an interconnected third-party computer.

- Encrypted data transmission. The capability to transmit EDI documents that have been encrypted by either sender or receiver.

- Immediate processing. The capability to process EDI transactions immediately so that the intended recipient can retrieve the message as soon as possible.

- Error-checking. Must support transmission of EDI documents using an error-checking telecommunications protocol.

- Immediate Connection. The capability to immediately establish a connection with a trading partner upon request and to send or receive data.

- International standards and protocols. The capability to support EDIFACT and other international standards.

- Transmission control protocol/internet protocol. The capability to support the transmission control protocol/internet protocol (TCP/IP) that the majority of Defense transportation activities use.

- Line speed conversion. The capability to support and convert multiple line speeds, including 2,400, 9,600, 14,400, and 19,200 bits per second.

- Multiple communications protocol conversion. The capability to support asynchronous; bisynchronous; Defense Information Systems Network (DISN) basic X.25; and system network architectures.

- Time-based dial-out. The capability to schedule a dial-out session with a VAN customer (trading partner) to deliver and receive data.

- Toll-free EDI VAN access. The capability to be accessed using a local or nationwide toll-free telephone call.

Security. In order to support current and future Defense Transportation EDI projects, a VAN must provide the following security services: (DoD, 1996: B-3)

- Encryption and authentication. The ability to encrypt and authenticate data using DoD security standards.

- Controlled VAN access. The ability to secure VAN access from unauthorized personnel.

Survivability. Due to the critical mission of the Military Services, the EDI VAN needs to be capable of operating during times of national crisis or natural disaster. In order to provide adequate survivability, the VAN must provide the following services: (DoD, 1996: B-3)

- Backup systems. The ability to maintain "hot standby" backup systems in the event the host computer fails.

- Disaster recovery plan. A documented procedure that permits the ongoing processing of EDI transactions when the host computer fails.

- Network redundancy. The automatic use of alternative routes within the telecommunications network when the network fails.

- Uninterruptable power supply. The availability of an uninterruptable power supply for the host computer, its backup systems, and all network hardware in the event of power failure.

Operational Facilities. In support of daily operations of the DTEDI program, a VAN needs to provide the following data recovery services and test facilities: (DoD, 1996: B-3 – B-4)

- Data recovery. The ability to restore EDI transactions to a mailbox for at least seven days after the origination of the transaction.

- Test facilities. The availability of facilities for testing hardware, software, and telecommunications protocols with multiple trading partners and networks.

Report Facilities. Because it monitors daily telecommunications traffic and forecasts future telecommunications requirements, the Defense transportation community monitors its usage of VANs. Therefore, the VAN provides the following information: (DoD, 1996: B-4)

- Transaction status history. The ability to provide transaction status messages including date and time stamps, throughout the life cycle of inbound and outbound transactions.

- Usage statistics. The availability of network usage statistics reports and network bills by document type, date, peak and off-peak usage times, and various other types of data.

Customer Support. As trading partners initiate new telecommunications links, manage existing links, and execute daily transmissions, they need access to customer support and other customer-related services to include: (DoD, 1996: B-4)

- Customer support hotline. The availability of customer service personnel 24 hours a day through a nationwide toll-free system.

- Lost data or delayed delivery notification. The capability to notify, by telephone, the sending trading partner that data have been lost or their delivery has been delayed.

- Installation support. The availability of training, consultation, and documentation for installation and set-up of EDI VAN access.

VAN System Operation

USTRANSCOM had two alternatives to solve its data incompatibility problem: develop an organic VAN capability, or outsource to an established company. There are three major disadvantages to developing an organic capability: (DoD, 1996: 6-4)

- Cost. With an organic system, the DoD must pay all fixed and variable costs associated with system operation. If the capability is outsourced, all VAN customers pay a portion of the contractor's fixed costs to operate the system.

44

- Technological Obsolescence. "The DoD has difficulty keeping pace with commercial industry advances in telecommunications standards and technology." Whatever system is used, periodic software and hardware upgrades must be accomplished to maintain a technological parity with the commercial sector. Since the DoD operates within the constraints of a two-year budget cycle, the DoD will typically have the most outdated equipment.

- Experience. The DoD has limited experience with EDI and therefore would expose USTRANSCOMs initiatives to a high degree of risk.

Faced with these disadvantages, the DoD initially used a third-party contractor supported VAN to provide the DoD's EDI interface requirements. As the DoD program continued to grow it was evident EDI was integral to all aspects of DoD operations and was sufficiently large to outweigh the disadvantages associated with developing an organic VAN capability. Due to the massive number of transactions conducted through EDI, the Defense Information Services Agency (DISA) and the Defense Logistics Agency (DLA) eventually established a DoD owned VAN.

The VAN communications architecture is easily understood. Figure 7 depicts the flow of data from commercial carriers through a DoD owned and operated VAN to GTN and its users. The commercial carriers, VAN, and DoD all operate their own systems. The commercial carriers are responsible for supplying data to the VAN as stipulated by the TPA. The VAN ensures data are in the proper format for GTN acceptance, and it also performs other required functions. GTN does not send any data back to the VAN. The only data flowing from GTN is to the GTN users. Finally, the last major flow of data consists of reports from the VAN to the commercial carriers. These reports provide feedback on data accuracy and transaction completion.

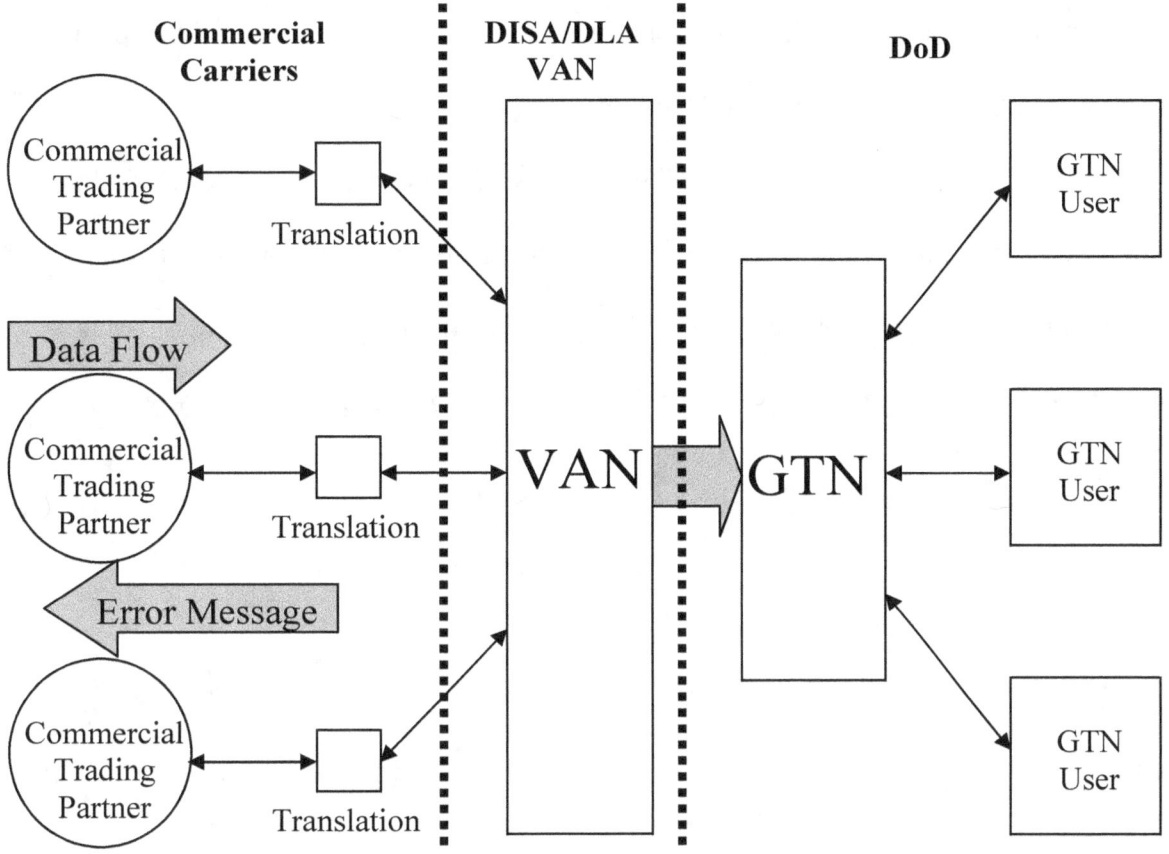

Figure 7. EDI VAN Communications Architecture

Chapter Summary

January 18, 1995 marked the beginning of USTRANSCOM's leadership role in the DoD EDI program. Since implementing the DTEDI Program, several methods have been used to capture source data for DoD purposes. It was determined early on that the use of a VAN was required to successfully join the DoD with its commercial trading partners. The VAN performs many important functions, but the most important is enabling electronic communications to be conducted between the DoD and the commercial business sector. Although it was initially advantageous to have a third party contractor operate the VAN, it soon became apparent that the DoD EDI operation was sufficiently large to produce its own economies of scale and therefore could be operated organically at a lower cost than once thought.

The basic architecture of the DTEDI process is not difficult to understand. In order for the system to work properly, it must successfully integrate four areas of the DTEDI process: tender submission, planning, movement, and payment. Each area is important in its own right, and is also critical to achieving ITV of commercially transported DoD assets.

V. Barriers to EDI Success

Introduction

There have been many successes in the DTEDI program. Since its inception, the DTEDI program has expanded to include business transactions with 28 commercial carriers; over 3 million transactions are conducted everyday solely using electronic means (Black, 2000). Because of EDI, the GTN is closer to its objective of attaining 100% visibility of all cargo and personnel being moved through the DTS system. But barriers exist that threaten to stall EDI initiatives preventing the system from achieving its full potential. This chapter discusses several barriers that threaten to limit the success of the DTEDI program and therefore threaten ITV initiatives.

What Are the Barriers?

In his 1994 Masters Thesis, Meier identified four barriers to DTEDI implementation. The barriers identified in the infancy stage of DTEDI are, as expected, associated with typical growing pains of any new system or technology. Meier identified the following as barriers to the efficient implementation of EDI within the DoD: (Meier, 1994: 113)

- Lack of knowledge and/or understanding

- Decentralization of effort

- Standardization

- Cost-benefit analysis and resourcing

As the DTEDI program has matured, barriers to continued growth have changed. USTRANSCOM addressed each of these barriers to implementation when it published the *DTEDI Program Implementation Plan* in 1996. Since taking command of DoD EDI efforts, USTRANSCOM has developed a considerable technological understanding of EDI capabilities and practices. In fact, EDI practices are used wherever they are able to improve existing paper-based processes. By appointing USTRANSCOM as lead agency for the DTEDI Program, the DoD centralized EDI efforts and ensured the development of a cohesive, systematic EDI effort.

Early in the DTEDI Program, USTRANSCOM recognized how critical data standardization was to overall EDI success. EDI does not work if separate computer systems cannot communicate, and standardized data sets using the ASC X12 convention are key to DTEDI success.

The final barrier identified by Meier concerned the difficulty with quantification of cost-benefits associated with EDI implementation. Of the three barriers identified by Meier, this is the only one that still exists. But, as the DTEDI program developed two new barriers to continued EDI success emerged: technology changeover, and incomplete data capture.

Cost-Benefit Analysis and Resourcing

A business lives or dies based on its profitability. If cost-benefit analysis does not reveal that implementing a specific program will increase profits through direct or indirect effects, then the program is discontinued or not even begun. The DoD does not have this same standard to measure success.

Because it is a not-for-profit organization, the DoD does not operate on a profit margin, and must use subjective, mission related measures to determine which programs should or should not be implemented. "The real obstacle is associated with the potential for subjectivity and the resulting difficulty in identifying what the actual (or anticipated) indirect benefits are, or will be" (Meier, 1994: 115).

Every year, the DoD must justify its intended budget to Congress. Since the DoD budget comprises the largest portion of federal discretionary funding, many legislators' view every dollar spent on defense as a dollar that could have been spent on some other social program. This congressional mentality forces the DoD to justify every dollar it intends to spend. The challenge the DoD has with procuring funding for EDI development is that the benefits of EDI are intangible: increased efficiency and effectiveness. Both are subjective measures of success. Adding to the challenge is justifying how much improvement is needed and what that improvement should cost. As a result, the DoD will have to continue its annual funding justification for EDI requirements. If funding is not granted at necessary levels, the EDI program will achieve a lower level of success.

Technology Changeover

It is estimated that computer speed doubles every few years. It is evident by examining local newspaper advertisements that the fastest computer purchased today will be easily outclassed within nine months to one year. This rapid technology changeover creates a unique challenge for the DoD and its EDI initiatives.

The business sector funds hardware upgrades within its own EDI system whenever such upgrades provide a cost effective business advantage or provide a capability which its customers demand. Because they are driven by a profit motive, businesses upgrade their communications and computer technologies much more quickly than does the DoD.

Again, the Federal budget process restricts the DoD from maintaining technological parity with its civilian trading partners. The DoD operates on a two-year budget cycle. This means it takes two years from identification of a budget requirement until that need is funded. To illustrate, in Fiscal Year (FY) 2000, the DoD is developing the budget it will submit to congress in FY 2001. When the Congress receives this budget, it takes another year before the budget is enacted into law. The result is that the DoD must look two years into the future and determine which programs to fund, and at what level. Because of the one-year technology changeover cycle, it is almost impossible for the DoD to keep up with the growth in technology, and with technology applications resident within the commercial sector.

Because EDI exploits advances in technology to produce an efficient and effective DTS, EDI hardware must be continuously upgraded to maintain parity with the commercial sector. Technology advancement is not only necessary for EDI development, but is also a barrier to future growth because of budget limitations.

Capturing All the Source Data

The final barrier affecting the success of DTEDI implementation is an inability to capture the data necessary to provide ITV of all commercially transported DoD assets. Experts at USTRANSCOM highlighted two primary reasons for incomplete data capture; they are inaccurate data, and incomplete EDI interfacing with the commercial transportation industry (Black, 2000a).

Inaccurate Data. As with any computer system, the data resident within GTN is only as good as the people and systems feeding the information. If data are not accurate when they are first entered, they will continue to be inaccurate until identified and fixed through human or computer intervention. Table 8 lists all commercial transportation carriers conducting EDI business transactions with the DoD during May 2000. The columns indicate two general types of errors, VAN errors and GTN fatal errors. Both types of errors result in unprocessed transactions requiring human intervention to correct the problem.

VAN errors indicate the number of transactions that reached the VAN but were not forwarded on to GTN. VAN errors occur when information such as a date or transportation control number is missing from the EDI transmission. VAN errors are usually caused by the shipper providing inadequate information to the carrier, and not by the VAN itself (Bowman, 2000a).

GTN fatal errors are caused by transactions that passed VAN scrutiny, but were still unable to be processed. A GTN fatal error results from improper information populating a data field such as a two-letter state identifier of XX instead of one of the fifty accepted abbreviations. Like VAN errors, GTN fatal errors result in shipment data that is not available to GTN users, and therefore greatly impacts ITV of commercially

transported DoD assets.

Table 8. EDI System Errors for May 2000
(Bowman, 2000)

Carrier	Total Transactions	VAN Errors	% VAN Errors	GTN Fatals	% GTN Fatals	Unprocessed Transactions
ABFS	35,781	0	-	4,337	12.12%	12.12%
AIPA	834	0	-	0	-	-
APLU	13,010	157	1.21%	2,454	**18.86%**	20.07%
BAGT	607	0	-	0	-	-
BNAF	11,354	0	-	178	1.57%	1.57%
CFWY	71,104	9	0.01%	4,142	5.83%	5.84%
CSXL	43,800	109	0.25%	356	0.81%	1.06%
CSXT	18,094	4,654	**25.72%**	1,483	8.20%	**33.92%**
DHL	185,341	11,416	6.16%	11,475	6.19%	12.35%
DIAB	1,059	5	0.47%	76	7.18%	7.65%
EWCF	8,343	1	0.01%	777	9.31%	9.33%
FDE	**1,584,395**	39,008	2.46%	**188,565**	11.90%	14.36%
GVTD	774	0	-	3	0.39%	-
HJBT	735	0	-	8	1.09%	1.09%
LRGR	632	0	-	0	-	-
LYKL	6,937	0	-	6	0.09%	0.09%
MATS	4,820	31	0.64%	217	4.50%	5.15%
MCET	241	1	0.41%	3	1.24%	1.66%
ODFL	806	0	-	37	4.59%	4.59%
OVNT	25,987	0	-	1,041	4.01%	4.01%
RDWY	56,772	0	-	34	0.06%	0.06%
SAII	261	0	-	1	0.38%	0.38%
TRIM	2,461	16	0.65%	76	3.09%	3.74%
TSMT	2,090	1	0.05%	156	7.46%	7.51%
UP	43,520	22	0.05%	1,773	4.07%	4.12%
VOSH	428	0	-	0	-	-
WHTT	174	4	2.30%	9	5.17%	7.47%
YFSY	30,245	0	-	3,217	10.64%	10.64%
TOTALS	**2,150,605**	**55,434**	**2.58%**	**220,424**	**10.25%**	**12.83%**

VAN and GTN fatal errors combined to cause an unprocessed transaction rate of

12.83 percent during May 2000(Bowman, 2000). This means that 13 of every 100 shipments transported via commercial means were not visible to DTS customers through GTN. Another interesting piece of information to note is the fact that air cargo shipments account for 83 percent of all DoD commercial movements. As would be expected, air carrier shipments cause a significant amount of error in the DTEDI system.

Table 9 shows only air carrier shipments for the month of May 2000 and the number of VAN errors and GTN fatal errors resulting in unprocessed shipments. According to Bowman, one reason air carriers contribute such a large number of errors to the DTEDI system is due to the reason for using air transportation. The DoD uses air movement when a

package or other piece of cargo must arrive at its final destination in a short period of time. These shipments move so quickly, they do not allow enough time for data correction prior to the shipment being delivered and subsequently closed.

Table 9. EDI System Errors for May 2000
(Bowman, 2000)

Carrier	Total Transactions	VAN Errors	% VAN Errors	GTN Fatals	% GTN Fatals	Unprocessed Transactions
BNAF	11,354	0	-	178	-	1.57%
DHL	185,341	11,416	6.16%	11,475	6.19%	12.35%
EWCF	8,343	1	0.01%	777	9.31%	9.33%
FDE	1,584,395	39,008	2.46%	188,565	11.90%	14.36%
TOTALS	1,789,433	50,425	2.82%	200,995	11.23%	14.05%

Incomplete Data Interfacing. Adding to data accuracy problems is the fact that the DTEDI system does not interface with all carrier transactions. In fact, the DTEDI program captures only 67 percent of all commercial DoD movements, accounting for over 3 million daily transactions (Heimerman, 2000). Many of the shipments that are not currently captured are overnight business package shipments. The rest of the shipments are transported by small commercial transportation companies that either do not have EDI capability, or the amount of DoD business conducted by these companies is too small to justify the expense associated with establishing a DTEDI link (Black, 2000a).

Air carrier shipments account for 83 percent of all daily commercial shipments. These shipments occur so quickly that data are typically not entered into any government system although they are accounted for through the carriers tracking system. The real debate is should this type of shipment be tracked by GTN? According to the *Defense ITV Integration Plan* ITV does not mean visibility of some shipments; ITV as set forth in the plan means visibility of all DoD shipments, unit equipment, and personnel moving throughout the DTS (DoD, 1996: 3-7). Can the DoD afford the expense associated with capturing data that are needed only for an overnight shipment? Does the DoD really need ITV of every overnight transaction?

Chapter Summary

Several barriers impact the ability of the DTEDI program to provide ITV of commercially transported DoD cargo. Throughout the brief history of the DTEDI program, several barriers have been overcome due to the detailed nature of the *DTEDI Program Implementation Plan.* Yet several barriers continue to degrade USTRANSCOM EDI efforts. If USTRANSCOM is going to achieve its goal of ITV of all DoD movements within the DTS, then barriers to EDI implementation must be removed.

VI. Conclusion

Overview

Operation Desert Storm marked a turning point in US National Defense Strategy. The US military could no longer plan on equipment and personnel being stationed near the battlefield prior to hostilities. The DoD was forced to rely on its transportation system to move all necessary cargo and personnel to the fight in a quick and efficient manner. The problem was that no capability existed to track a shipment's location or status while in the DTS and thus inefficiencies plagued the system. Added to this, the DoD was now more dependent upon the commercial sector for transportation needs than it had ever been before and therefore had little control of much of its own equipment and personnel.

In this chapter, the investigative questions introduced in Chapter I are discussed. The answers are derived from information presented throughout this research paper.

Investigative Questions

Question 1. The first step in answering the research question is to provide the reader with a fundamental understanding of Electronic Data Interchange and how it is used in the civilian sector. The first investigative question that must be answered then is what is Electronic Data Interchange?

Electronic Data Interchange is not a specific system; it is an application of existing and emerging technologies that provides for the sharing of data between organizations. Officially, EDI is the computer-to-computer exchange of data from common business documents using standard data formats.

EDI offers numerous advantages over traditional paper-based communications systems. Benefits include cost savings, data accuracy, and communications speed. Given today's high technology business environment, EDI is a concept whose time has arrived.

Question 2. Another integral aspect of the research question is the concept of In-transit Visibility. Adding a fundamental understanding of EDI to an understanding of ITV provides the basic tools for understanding the larger issues confronting USTRANSCOM ITV initiatives. Therefore, the second investigative question is what is In-transit Visibility, and how does the Global Transportation Network provide it?

Following Operation Desert Storm, the Deputy Under Secretary of Defense (Logistics), established the requirement for the DoD to develop a system which could maintain visibility of all assets, this concept was known as Total Asset Visibility (TAV). An integral part of TAV is the concept of ITV. The *Defense In-transit Visibility Plan* defines ITV as

> The ability to track the identity, status, and location of DoD unit and non-unit cargo (excluding bulk petroleum, oils, and lubricants); passengers; medical patients; and personal property from origin to the consignee or destination designated by the CINCs, Military Services, or Defense agencies, during peace, contingencies, and war.

Providing ITV required the development of a new computer network known as the Global Transportation Network. GTN is a collection of information from 25 different computer systems allowing cross-service shipment tracking. GTN is the backbone of USTRANSCOM's ITV initiatives.

Question 3. In the past, poor quality data and the absence of timely data, each contributed adversely to an inadequate ITV system. EDI offers the capability to correct these shortcomings and provide ITV of DoD's commercial movements via GTN. Does the DoD need ITV of commercial movements, and therefore need EDI for DTS effectiveness?

The DoD has a genuine operational requirement for EDI. The military services needed commercial sector augmentation during Desert Storm to move the vast quantities of troops and equipment required of the Iraqi invasion. Since Desert Storm, the military force has shrunk by another 30 percent, contributing to the DoD dependence upon commercial carriers for wartime troop movements. But, with more cargo moving by commercial means, the DoD has a tough job maintaining ITV of all its assets.

EDI offers a solution to the DoD. EDI technology can provide a means for the DoD to continue to receive shipment status reports on its valuable equipment. Not only does EDI provide a way for the DoD to continue to have ITV of its in-transit assets, but it is also the preferred method of conducting business with most transportation companies.

Question 4. Even after GTN is fully developed and required system interfaces are in place, the risk of inadequate ITV information is still present. If the DoD is going to use EDI to facilitate ITV of commercially transported DoD assets; a detailed plan must be established describing a systematic approach to EDI implementation. What is the current plan for Defense Transportation EDI (DTEDI) implementation?

January 18, 1995 marked the beginning of USTRANSCOM's leadership role in the DoD EDI program. It was determined early on that the use of a Value Added Network was required to successfully join the DoD with its commercial trading partners.

58

The VAN performs many important functions, but the most important is enabling electronic communications to be conducted between the DoD and the commercial business sector. Although it was initially advantageous to have a third party contractor operate the VAN, it became apparent early on that the DoD EDI operation was sufficiently large to produce its own economies of scale and therefore could be operated organically at a lower cost than once thought.

The basic architecture of the DTEDI process is not difficult to understand. For the system to work properly, it must successfully integrate four areas of the DTEDI process: tender submission, planning, movement, and payment. Each area is important in its own right and is critical to achieving ITV of commercially transported DoD assets.

The *DTEDI Program Implementation Plan* is not a finished work. Although the written document has not changed since its inception in June 1996, the working plan has evolved with advances in technology, and has grown to accommodate changing mission requirements.

Question 5. The final investigative question addresses the ability of the DTEDI program to affect ITV. What are the barriers affecting Electronic Data Interchange implementation?

As with any new system, there are several barriers that must be overcome if EDI is going to achieve it's intended success. According to USTRANSCOM's *DTEDI Program Implementation Plan*, EDI will eventually provide visibility of all commercially transported DoD assets. But, for complete visibility of all intransit DoD assets to become a reality, three key barriers must be overcome.

First, the DoD must find a way to collect all data required by the VAN and GTN. Second, EDI hardware must be upgraded as technology improves thus allowing the DTEDI program to maintain technological parity with commercial trading partners. The third barrier, effective cost analysis and resourcing, has been a barrier since DTEDI program inception. Although each barrier was presented as a discrete impediment, a common thread links each. The common element between the three is funding. All EDI barriers could be greatly reduced if DTEDI initiatives received proper funding.

Research Paper Summary

The DTEDI program is a complex program designed to join the DoD with its commercial trading partners. Ideally, EDI will revolutionize the way in which the DoD conducts business by eliminating as many paper-based transactions as possible. Numerous advantages are associated with EDI implementation; one advantage is an ability to capture commercial shipment data and provide ITV of commercially transported DoD cargo and personnel. The success of Operation Desert Storm was contingent upon commercial transportation assets. Since Operation Desert Storm, the DoD has increased its reliance upon those assets.

If the DoD is going to achieve its goal of 100 percent ITV of DoD movements within the DTS, then barriers to EDI implementation must be removed. If these barriers are to be reduced or removed, proper funding must be supplied enabling EDI to mature and grow with operational demands. Alleviation of budgeting pressure could occur through budget reform legislation, or by improving DoD needs forecasting. No matter how the barriers are lifted, improved EDI capabilities will greatly improve DTS operation.

Appendix A

System descriptions

ADANS   =   Airlift Deployment Analysis System (AMC)

A migration system that captures airlift planning requirements and will interface with GTN. It prepares movement tables and schedules for operation plans, operation orders, channel requirements, and tanker schedules. It assists in transportation feasibility analyses. The name will change to the Consolidated Air Mobility Planning System (CAMPS).

AMS   =   Asset Management System (MTMC)

A developing GTN Interface system that automates the management of the DoD Interchange Freight Car Fleet and the Common User Container Fleet. It replaces two legacy systems: Defense Rail Interchange Fleet System and Joint Container Control System.

BROKER   =   Broker (AMC)

Broker provides automated support for maintenance activities at fixed and key en route strategic airlift locations. Broker is the maintenance system for the C-5, C-141, KC-10, KC-135 and C-17 aircraft, and has provisions to accommodate other transient aircraft. The system has a central computer at Tinker AFB Data Service Center (TDSC).
The Broker system will provide compatible physical and functional connectivity between C2IPS, GTN, and Broker. C2IPS, GTN, and Broker will share data through automated traffic exchanged via Broker. Broker provides routing to the appropriate system and translates and reformats passed data items as needed for input to the receiving system. The data passed from Broker to GTN will be in AMC Command and Control Interface Design Document (C2IDD) format USMTF messages.
As a source system for GTN, Broker will provide maintenance status information on AMC and other aircraft.

CAPS II = Consolidated Aerial Port System II (AMC)

The current real-time system that carries out local passenger and cargo processing functions at AMC's aerial ports. This system allows each aerial port to communicate with Headquarters AMC transportation systems and other aerial ports. It has three applications: Second Generation Passenger Reservation and Check-in System, Cargo, and Aerial Port Automated Command and Control System. CAPS II interfaces with the GTN. It is one of the systems scheduled to be replaced by GATES.

CEDI VAN/TPS = Commercial EDI Value Added Network/Transaction Processing Subsystem (CSX)

As a source system for GTN, the CEDI VAN/TPS provides transaction data on movement events reported by the commercial transportation industry. The CEDI VAN/TPS interface data allows GTN to expand the visibility of DoD cargo to include movement status information for Defense material moving on air, motor, rail, and ocean commercial carriers. The CEDI VAN/TPS primary site is located at CSX (CSX) in Jacksonville, Florida.

GTN shall interface with CEDI VAN/TPS. CEDI VAN/TPS is a commercial unclassified system designed to provide visibility of commercial cargo movement.

CFM = CONUS Freight Management (MTMC)

A migration system scheduled to interface with GTN. It automates shipment planning and document preparation for government bill of lading (GBL) shipments. Through the use of electronic data interchange (EDI) techniques, it exchanges shipment information with users from transportation offices, carriers, and the Defense Finance and Accounting Service.

The CFM Field Module, which is replacing TRAMS, will support vendor shipments with delivery terms of FOB origin, by processing shipment data and creating GBL's.

CMOS = Cargo Movement Operations System (USAF)

The Air Force's TC AIMS that automates base-level cargo movement processes and provides transportation movement officers with current unit movement data. TC AIMS II is the planned replacement for this system.

DAASC	=	Defense Automated Addressing System Center (DLA)
		DAASC is the DLA's unclassified system for automatically routing MILSTRIP transactions among customers, suppliers, depots, and shipping activities. DAASC will supply GTN information on the status of requisitions ordered via MILSTRIP. As a source data system for GTN, DAASC will interface with GTN for data concerning supply requisitions and the reported movement status of the items requisitioned, to include initial shipment by a depot, shipment by a CCP and final receipt by the consignee. DAASC will provide GTN information regarding requisitions being processed by the Defense Supply System that require overseas shipment. As a customer system for GTN, DAASC will receive nodal date/time information associated with DAASC requisitions.
DTTS	=	Defense Transportation Tracking System (DoD/USN/MTMC)
		A GTN interface system that monitors all CONUS arms, ammunition, and explosives shipment moving by truck. It performs this task using a commercial satellite tracking surveillance service, which provides DTTS with truck location reports, intransit truck status changes, and emergency situation notifications.
DTTS-E	=	Defense Transportation Tracking System – Europe (DoD/USN/MTMC)
		As a source system for GTN, DTTS-E will interface with GTN to provide satellite-tracking data from the QualComm Regional Dispatch/Monitor Station. DTTS-E data (subject to data quality constraints and the extent of the QualComm Satellite Tracking application) provides the location of organic vehicle assets equipped with the European QualComm Satellite Tracking transponders.
GATES	=	Global Air Transportation Execution System (AMC)
		A GTN interface system under development that will replace and assume the functions of HOST, PRAMS, CAPS II, DCAPS and their subsystems.
GCCS	=	Global Command and Control System (JCS)
		A future replacement system for the JOPES. It will provide time-phased force deployment data and movement requirements to GTN.

GDSS = Global Decision Support System (AMC)

A GTN interface system that provides aircraft scheduling and execution information. An AMC migration system that records and displays airlift schedules, aircraft arrivals and departures, and limited aircraft status. It provides executive-level decision support. An original GTN prototype interface system.

GOPAX = Group Operational Passenger System (MTMC)

A GTN interface system that provides operational and management information support in arranging group/unit movement transportation by bus, rail, or air. It will automate these Headquarters MTMC functions and provide both installation transportation office/traffic management office and carrier automated interface.

GTN = Global Transportation Network (USTRANSCOM)

A system that provides the automated support that USTRANSCOM and its components need to carryout their global transportation management responsibilities. It provides the integrated transportation data necessary to accomplish transportation planning, command and control, and patient movement. It also provides DoD-wide intransit visibility of units, passengers, and cargo during peace and war.

IBS = Integrated Booking System (MTMC)

A new MTMC traffic management system that will interface with GTN. It registers cargo for sealift, provide schedules for unit arrival at ports, and issue port calls to units. IBS will include the functionality of Military Export Traffic System II (METS II) and ASPUR.

IC3 = Integrated Command, Control, and Communications System (MSC)

The Military Sealift Command's command, control, and communications system. It will provide vessel schedules and locations. IC3 replaces the Vessel Information Planning and Analysis System (VIPS). IC3 will interface with GTN and IBS.

JALIS = Joint Air Logistics Information System (USN)

A developing joint system that will be used to schedule operational support aircraft, providing ITV of requirements and missions.

JOPES   =   Joint Operations Planning and Execution System (JCS)

The foundation of DoD's conventional command and control system, which comprises policies, procedures, and reporting systems supported by automation. It is used to monitor, plan and execute mobilization, deployment, employment, and sustainment activities in peace, exercises, crises, and war. It will be replaced by GCCS, which will provide Time Phased Force Deployment Data and movement requirements to GTN.

JTAV   =   Joint Total Asset Visibility (DoD)

LIA Regional   =   Logistics Integration Agency's (LIA)-Regional Servers
Servers

As a source system for GTN, LIA-Regional Servers will interface with GTN to provide visibility of cargo from the point of origin. The RF Tags are placed on containers, pallets, and equipment and the RF Tag interrogators are positioned at key choke points and transportation nodes such as airfields, container or pallet holding areas, rail heads, gates, and bridges. The data is updated as the tag-equipped container progresses from its point of origin to its destination moving past RF Tag interrogators that report the time and location of the interrogated RF Tag. GTN shall interface with LIA-Regional Servers. LIA-Regional Servers' Radio Frequency (RF) Tag systems provide near-real time remote monitoring, tracking, and location of forces and equipment.

TC ACCIS   =   Transportation Coordinator's Automated Command and Control Information System (USA)

The Army TC Aims that is used to plan and execute unit deployments and redeployments worldwide, communicate data to the U.S. Forces Command for updating JOPES, and communicate data to MTMC for port operations and load planning. It generates air load plans, air cargo manifests, unit movement data, convoy march tables and clearance requests, rail load plans, bills of lading, and bar-code labels. TC AIMS II is the planned replacement for this system.

TCAIMS II   =   Transportation Coordinator's Automated Information for Movement System II (USA)

A joint system being developed by the Army to replace the Military Services' TC AIMS family of systems. It automates the planning, organizing, coordinating, and controlling of unit-related deployment activities. It also permits transportation offices to maintain an automated database of current unit movement data. It will also provide the theater of operations with a joint theater transportation system capability.

TRAC2ES   =   TRANSCOM Regulating and Command and Control Evacuation System (USTRANSCOM)

A command and control system that provides for global patient movement and regulating. It also provides patient intransit visibility, monitors critical patient medical equipment pools, and assists in roundtrip transportation of patient attendants. Interface with GTN is scheduled by January 1999.

WPS   =   Worldwide Port System (MTMC)

The port operating system being fielded for military ocean terminals, Navy port activities, Army terminal units, and automated cargo documentation detachments.

Acronym List

ADANS	AMC Deployment Analysis System
AFB	Air Force Base
AFIT	Air Force Institute of Technology
AIT	Automatic Identification Technology
AMC	Air Mobility Command
AMS	Asset Management System
ANSI	American National Standards Institute
APLU	American Presidents Lines
ASC	Accredited Standard Committee
AU	Air University
BAGT	Baggett Transportation
BANF	BAX Global
CAPS II	Consolidated Aerial Port System II
CBL	Commercial Bill of Lading
CEDI	Commercial Electronic Data Interchange
CFM	CONUS Freight Management
CFWY	Consolidated Freightways
CINC	Commander in Chief
CMDS	Commands
CMOS	Cargo Movement Operations System
CONUS	Continental United States
CRAF	Civil Reserve Air Fleet
CSL	Computer Systems Laboratory
CSXL	CSX Lines
CSXT	CSX Transportation
DAASC	Defense Automatic Addressing System
DFAS-IN	Defense Finance and Accounting Service – Indianapolis
DHL	DHL Worldwide Express
DIAB	Diablo Transport, Inc.
DISA	Defense Information System Agency
DISA	Defense Information Systems Agency
DISN	Defense Information Systems Network
DLA	Defense Logistics Agency
DoD	Department of Defense
DTEDI	Defense Transportation Electronic Data Interchange
DTIC	Defense Technical Information Center

DTRS	Defense Transportation Payment System
DTS	Defense Transportation System
DTS	Defense Transportation System
DTTS	Defense Transportation Tracking System
DTTS-E	Defense Transportation System – Europe
DUSD(L)	Deputy Under Secretary of Defense for Logistics
EDI	Electronic Data Interchange
EDIFACT	EDI for Administration, Commerce, and Transport
EFT	Electronic Fund Transfer
ESI	External System Interface Project
EWCF	Emery Worldwide Consolidated Freight
FDE	Federal Express
FedEx	Federal Express
FOC	Future Operational Concept
FY	Fiscal Year
GAO	Government Accounting Office
GATES	Global Air Transportation Execution System
GBL	Government Bill of Lading
GCCS	Global Command and Control System
GDSS	Global Decision Support System
GOPAX	Group Operational Passenger System
GSA	Government Services Agency
GT	Guaranteed Traffic
GTN	Global Transportation Network
GVTD	Green Valley Transportation
HJBT	JB Hunt Transportation
HQ	Headquarters
IBS	Integrated Booking System
IC3	Integrated Command, Control, and Communications System
IGTN	Interactive Global Transportation Network
ITV	In-transit Visibility
JALIS	Joint Air Logistics Information Support System
JCS	Joint Chiefs of Staff
JICTRANS	Joint Intelligence Center USTRANSCOM
JOPES	Joint Operations Planning and Execution System
JTAV	Joint Total Asset Visibility
LIA	Logistics Integration Agency
LRGR	Ladstar Ranger

LYKL	Lykes Lines Limited
MATS	Matson Navigation
MCET	Mercer Transportation Company
MS	Masters
MSC	Military Sealift Command
MTMC	Military Traffic Management Command
NMCC	National Military Command Center
ODFL	Old Dominion Freight Lines
OVNT	Overnite Transportation
POD	Port of Deembarkation
POE	Port of Embarkation
RDWY	Roadway Express
S	Secret
SAII	SurfAir Incorporated
ST	Short Tons
TACC	Tanker Airlift Control Center
TAV	Total Asset Visibility
TC ACCIS	Transportation Coordinator's Automated Command and Control Information System
TCAIMS II	Transportation Coordinator's Automated Information for Movement System II
TCMD	Transportation Control and Movement Documents
TCP/IP	Transmission Control Protocol/Internet Protocol
TDCC	Transportation Data Coordinating Committee
TPA	Trading Partner Agreement
TPS	Transaction Processing Subsystem
TRAC2ES	TRANSCOM Regulating and Command Control Evacuation System
TRIM	Trism Specialized Carriers
TSMT	Tri-State Motor Transit Company
U	Unclassified
UCS	Uniform Communications Standard
UP	Union Pacific Railroad
UPS	United Parcel Service
USAF	United States Air Force
USCENTCOM	United States Central Command
USTC	United States Transportation Command
USTRANSCOM	United States Transportation Command

VAN	Value Added Network
VOSH	Van Ommeren Shipping
WHTT	C.I. Whitten
WPS	Worldwide Port System
Y2K	Year 2000
YFSY	Yellow Freight

Bibliography

Barkley, Don. United States Transportation Command, J-4, Scott AFB IL. Personal Correspondence. 13 August 1997.

Black, Thomas. United States Transportation Command, J-4, Scott AFB IL. Official Correspondence. 27 April 2000

Black, Thomas, Bruce Bowman, Jim Donovan and Ron Freed. United States Transportation Command, J-4, Scott AFB IL. Personal Interview. 5 May 2000a.

Bowman, Bruce. DynCorp Representative, contractor to Electronic Data Interchange Branch, United States Transportation Command, J-3, Scott AFB IL. *April 2000 EDI Data Statistics*. 5 May 2000.

Bowman, Bruce. DynCorp Representative, contractor to Electronic Data Interchange Branch, United States Transportation Command, J-3, Scott AFB IL. Personal Interview. 2 June 2000a.

Department of Defense (DoD). *Defense In-transit Visibility Integration Plan*. Washington: Government Printing Office, February, 1995a.

-----. *Defense Transportation EDI Program Implementation Plan*. Washington: Government Printing Office, June 1996.

Emmelhainz, Margaret A. EDI: A Total Management Guide (Second Edition). New York: Van Nostrand Reinhold, 1993.

Griffin, Ricky W. Management (Sixth Edition). New York: Houghton Mifflin Company, 1999.

Government Accounting Office (GAO). Military Capabilities and Readiness. Strategic Objective Plan: 2000 – 2002. Washington: Government Printing Office, 2000.

Hardcastle, T. P., EDI Planning and Implementation Guide, Logistics Management Institute, Report DL203RDI, August 1992.

Headquarters Air Mobility Command (HQ AMC). Command Data Book. Scott AFB IL: May 1999.

Heimerman. United States Transportation Command, J-4, Scott AFB IL. Official Correspondence. 28 April 2000.

Hinge, K. C. Electronic Data Interchange, From Understanding to Implementation. AMA Membership Publications Division, 1988.

HQ AMC TACC/XOO. "Kosovo International Humanitarian Support Missions." Electronic Message. 202000Z, May 1999.

Jones, Lori. Chief, In-transit Visibility Branch, United States Transportation Command, J-4, Scott AFB IL. Electronic Mail. 5 May 2000.

Lambert, Douglas M. and James R. Stock. Strategic Logistics Management (Third Edition). Boston: McGraw-Hill Book Company, 1993.

Matthews, James K. and Cora J. Holt. "So Many, So Much, So Far, So Fast: United States Transportation Command and Strategic Deployment for Operation Desert Shield/Desert Storm," Research Center: United States Transportation Command, Scott AFB IL and Joint History Office: Office of the Chairman of the Joint Chiefs of Staff, May 1996.

MacKeen, Richard. Planner, In-transit Visibility Branch, United States Transportation Command, J-4, Scott AFB IL. Personal Interview. 20 September 1999.

Meier, John G. The Implementation of Electronic Data Interchange (EDI) With Defense Transportation Operations. MS thesis. Naval Post Graduate School, Monterey, CA, March 1994.

Miller, James M. (1996). Intransit Visibility: Capturing All the Source Data. MS thesis, AFIT/GMO/LAP/96J-5. School of Logistics and Acquisition Management, Air Force Institute of Technology (AU), Wright-Patterson Air Force Base, Ohio, May 1996 (ADA309719).

Naisbitt, John. Input EDI Reporter. Quote. November 1988.

Payne, Judith E. and Robert H. Anderson. Using Electronic Commerce to Enhance Defense Logistics. Santa Monica CA. Rand, 1991.

Robertson, Charles T., JR. Commander in Chief, USTRANSCOM, Scott AFB, IL. Memorandum. 13 August 1999.

Sutton, Mathias, J. "The Role of Electronic Data Interchange in the Transportation Industry," Defense Transportation Journal, 53: 10-12 (August 1997).

Title 41 of the Code of Federal Regulations, Part 101-41, 1 July 1992.

United States Transportation Command (USTRANSCOM). GTN System Specification. USTRANSCOM Publication 171-1.3.1AC, Revision A. 30 April 1999.

Wolford, Dean A. <u>Improved Visibility Within the Air Force ITV System</u>. MS thesis, AFIT/GMO/LAL/96N-15. School of Logistics and Acquisition Management, Air Force Institute of Technology (AU), Wright-Patterson Air Force Base, Ohio, November 1996.